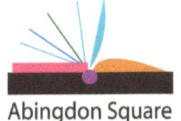

Abingdon Square

463 West St. #G122
NY, NY 10014
212.691.2543
www.abingdonsquarepublishing.com

PUBLISHED ON THE OCCASION

Gregory Crane
Drawings 1979 - 2009
April 29 - May 30, 2009

CHERYL PELAVIN
FINE ARTS, LLC

13 Jay Street, New York, NY 10013
212-925-9424
www.cherylpelavin.com

Design by Brian Pilliod

Gregory Crane, *Drawings 1979 - 2009*
is published by Abingdon Square Publishing

ISBN 978-0-9823480-0-0
Library of Congress Control Number: 2009925375

First Printing: April 2009
Printed in the United States of America

Special thanks to Brian Pilliod

Gregory Crane would like to thank his wife June, his sons
Lucus & Evan, Mike & Ann Beug, Cheryl Pelavin,
Brian Douglass, Trevor Winkfield, Simon Lane and Carl Little.

on cover: *Ripe Apple with View of Underground (detail)*, 1991-2, Chalk and Conte Crayon on Paper, 22 x 30 inches

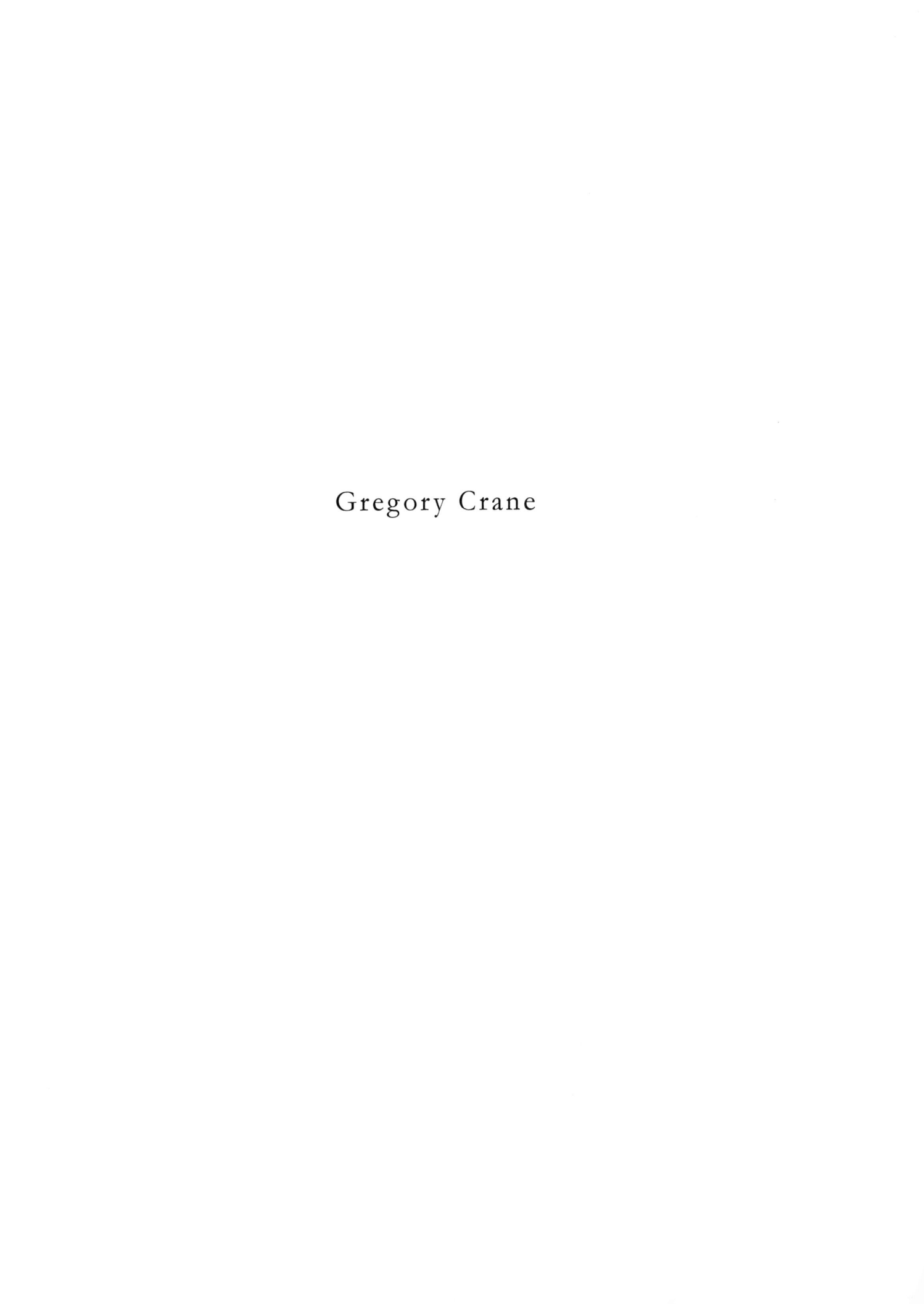

Gregory Crane

Gregory Crane

Drawings 1979 - 2009

April 29 - May 30, 2009

for June, Lucas & Evan

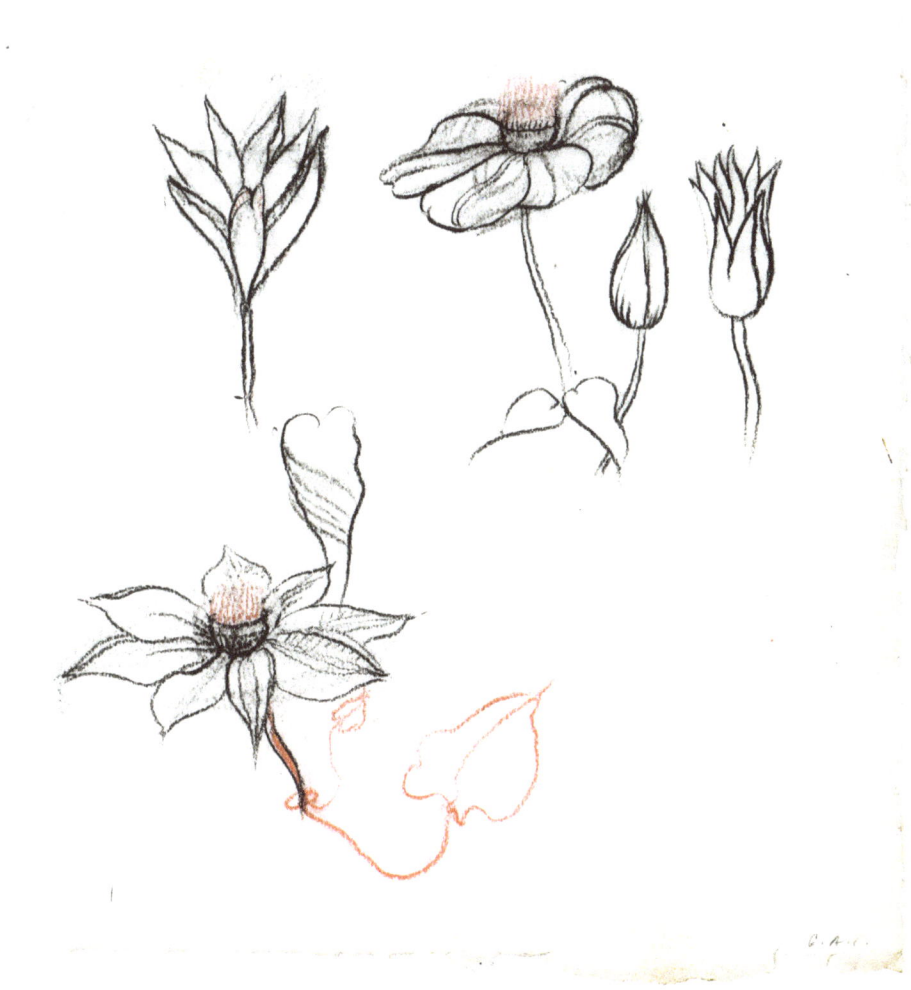

TOWN AND COUNTRY
by Trevor Winkfield, 2009

There are as many ways to depict a landscape as there are landscape painters. This is understood from the outset, no doubt. But one of the chief ways we can divide this diverse group into two distinct camps, at least to my mind, is to pile them onto a train well known for its "scenic route" and see what happens. The vast majority will automatically gravitate towards that side of the carriage which promises the best vantage point for uninterrupted views of the winding river, its yachts, distant shore, sunlit forest and snow-capped mountains. The other group of painters huddle on the opposite side of the carriage, there to scrutinize close up a more local landscape: the sloping embankment with its distant chimney stacks and abandoned warehouses, ramshackle tool sheds on parched grass strewn with mildewed bottles, pulped newspapers, grimy plastic bags and mile upon mile of metal fencing sagging under the suffocating weight of parasitic vegetation. On the branches of trees, old chairs and metal wagon wheels. One might class the landscapists who opted for the scenic side as Romantics, whilst those relegated to the opposite side are surely the true Visionaries.

Left or right, both seating's are, of course, legitimate. But lucky are those landscape painters who, like Gregory Crane, can look both ways at once. These two ways of looking can also be applied in a very obvious way to Crane's drawings ... as indeed they can to those of most artists. By which I mean that Crane produces both highly finished drawings and other, more notational studies, the latter rarely seen outside the artist's studio, intended as they are for his own guidance. Both serve the function of laboratory tests for subsequent paintings, and neither tries to eradicate signs of struggle. Or, as Crane himself has stated, "drawing is the heart and soul, the anatomy of what might become a painting."

It's not without relevance that Crane grew up on the family farm on the Olympic peninsula of North West Washington State, and has spent most of his creative life in a Brooklyn town house, just beyond the Gowanus Canal, within sight, sound and smell of Manhattan. His laboratory (by which I mean his head) has thus had the benefit of both rural and urban influences, both the fecundity and the muddle of life. This admixture was of the kind Thoreau obviously enjoyed during his supposed "isolation" at Walden Pond, which took place barely two miles from the bustling center of Concord. Crane in his own way has pursued this "best of both worlds" ideal. Though he's ranged far and wide in pursuit of motifs (from southern Vermont and upstate New York, to his native Washington State and Idaho), he's also, like so many other artists, found Paradise closer to home. For behind his house is a lovingly tended family garden which provides him year-round with an accessible supply of motifs. In Summer, flowers and plants bloom in profusion. In Winter, the garden's "anatomy" can be seen. Gone to seed, its outlines expose bedraggled trellises, gimcrack sheds, a wheelbarrow full of expiring plants, and overgrown paths dotted with sundry bushes belonging to the wilder shores of science fiction. Crane utilizes both versions.

Paradoxically his garden's domestic scale and location enables him not to confront nature, like some bombastic Frederick Church, but to insinuate himself into it, like a benevolent Samuel Palmer. (One might also notice the hidden influence of Dutch School favorites such as Adrien Brouwer, Phillips Konnick and Hercules Seghers ... and deeper yet, influences from the Bay Area figurative painters may still be detected.) To coax nature to do his bidding, Crane corrals a rich array of marks (usually in black chalk or sepia, in conte crayon, ink or pencil), which if not quite encyclopedic in range do, at least, provide him with a viable alphabet: tender tappings, strokes, wisps and surreptitious erasures are cross-bred with various scourings, jabs and skimming's to weave what amounts to that curious hybrid, elegiac expressionism. And just as Crane can use his stick of crayon as though it's a garden implement, so at other times his crayon can serve as a barometer, gauging the temperature of the terrain it's depicting. At other times, crayons are used like sculptural tools to mould a shape into a relief (I'm thinking in particular of one sculptural drawing showing the globular head of a cardamom plant, where the insistent carved probing via a pen nib end up making the prickly head look as threatening as a hand grenade). Like seashells held to the ear, such drawings deceive and convince at the same time.

Rarely does Crane allow human figures to intrude in his landscapes ... just the effect they've had upon it (though like most modern landscape painters, he no doubt fully accepts the medieval correlation between humans and the earth: bones as the equivalent of rocks, hair like grass, breath like the wind). When figures appear, they're glimpsed as phantoms: here eyes glare out of the darkness, and over there, elusive watchers stare from afar.

But by no means is all darkness and mystery; far from it. For though nature may have its nocturnal secrets, Crane's brand is outrageously bucolic too, as livable a region as any this side of ... well, Paradise. That both – the dark and the lighter moods of nature – can peacefully coexist on the same graphic plane is another of Crane's pleasures, and so typical of his dual vision.

Most curious of all, given that Crane is one of the most accomplished colorists of his generation, is the realization that all this is limned in the strictest monochrome, with barely a hint of color intruding to distract us from our intense concentration.

Cardamon Plant, 1995, Ink on Paper, 13 x 10 inches

cardiman

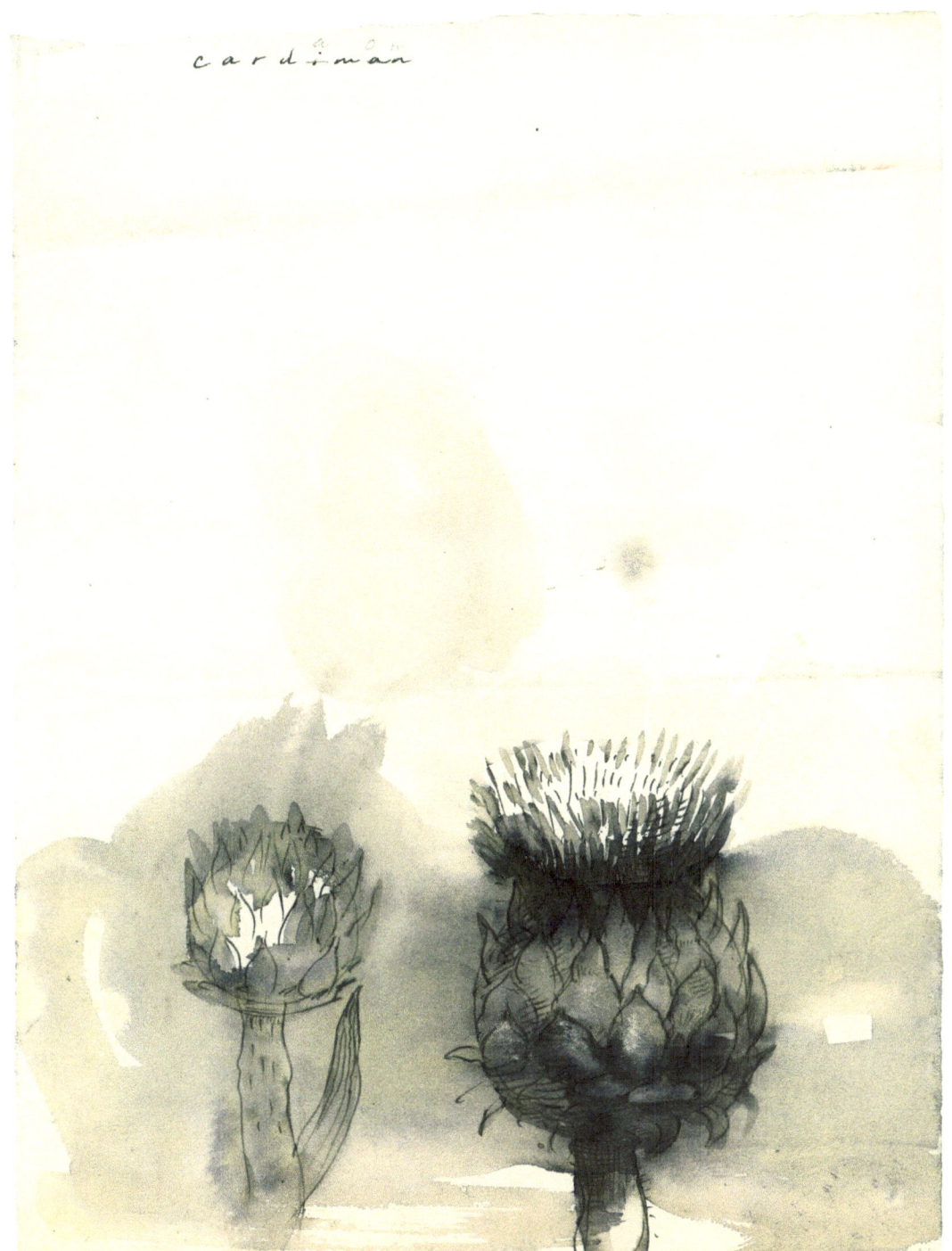

Gregory Crane is in the habit of being discovered. While that burdensome rock of fashion will always roll back to the foot of the mountain so that Sisyphus has to start all over again, Mr. Crane simply continues to do what he has always done, executing his work with extraordinary skill and consistency of purpose, free of the constraints suggested by a capricious age, the nagging distinction, for example, between art photography and photographic art, or the dreaded Conceptualism, Marcel`s joke at the Master`s expense, the promotion of the object through the demotion of the pencil. No, the true artist works in a true sphere, independent, oblivious to all but the formal, aesthetic demands created by the transposition of a tri-dimensional world onto a flat surface, an activity as old as the hills, or at least as old as the one on which Sisyphus was condemned to pound as a result of his tiff with Zeus.

Indifferent to the cyclical torture of fashion and of critical whimsy, Crane adheres to the methodology - observation, composition, draughtsmanship - of one driven to recreate his surroundings, rather than litter them with the bits and bobs that constitute subject matter in what is called the art world but which I prefer to call the art club, a strange institution whose members, seeking comfort in numbers, become, to the numberless spectator, numberless in repetition. Singular and happily so, Crane strides forth in a straight line since the beginnings of his productivity, offering countless shades and sides to the land and cityscape that so wholly envelop him, the be all and end all of a curiosity sharpened with time, coupled with wit. There are always precursors, eclecticism is ineluctable in a discipline honed through the ages, one simply has to choose the right path, the right way forward.

His work reveals diverse lineage. He has mentioned Rembrandt and Breughel, along with American antecedents, Ryder, Innes and Blakelocke. Blake, Samuel Palmer and Joan Miró spring to mind, the latter`s identification and depiction of isolated objects in a reinvented universe so apt a symbol of the human condition, somehow resonating with the outlandish Bosch, of whom Crane has spoken.

Hard to pin down exactly? Naturally. In an interview we did some fifteen years ago, Crane spoke of the "pure intoxication" of his chosen art. When pressed on the matter, he suggested he might be a "meta-proto-arch-primal-real-realist." Well, that should keep the Sisyphean school of fashion quiet, for this season at least.

Simon Lane, 2009

Willow at Angle, 1995, Charcoal and Conte Crayon on Paper, 11 x 15 inches

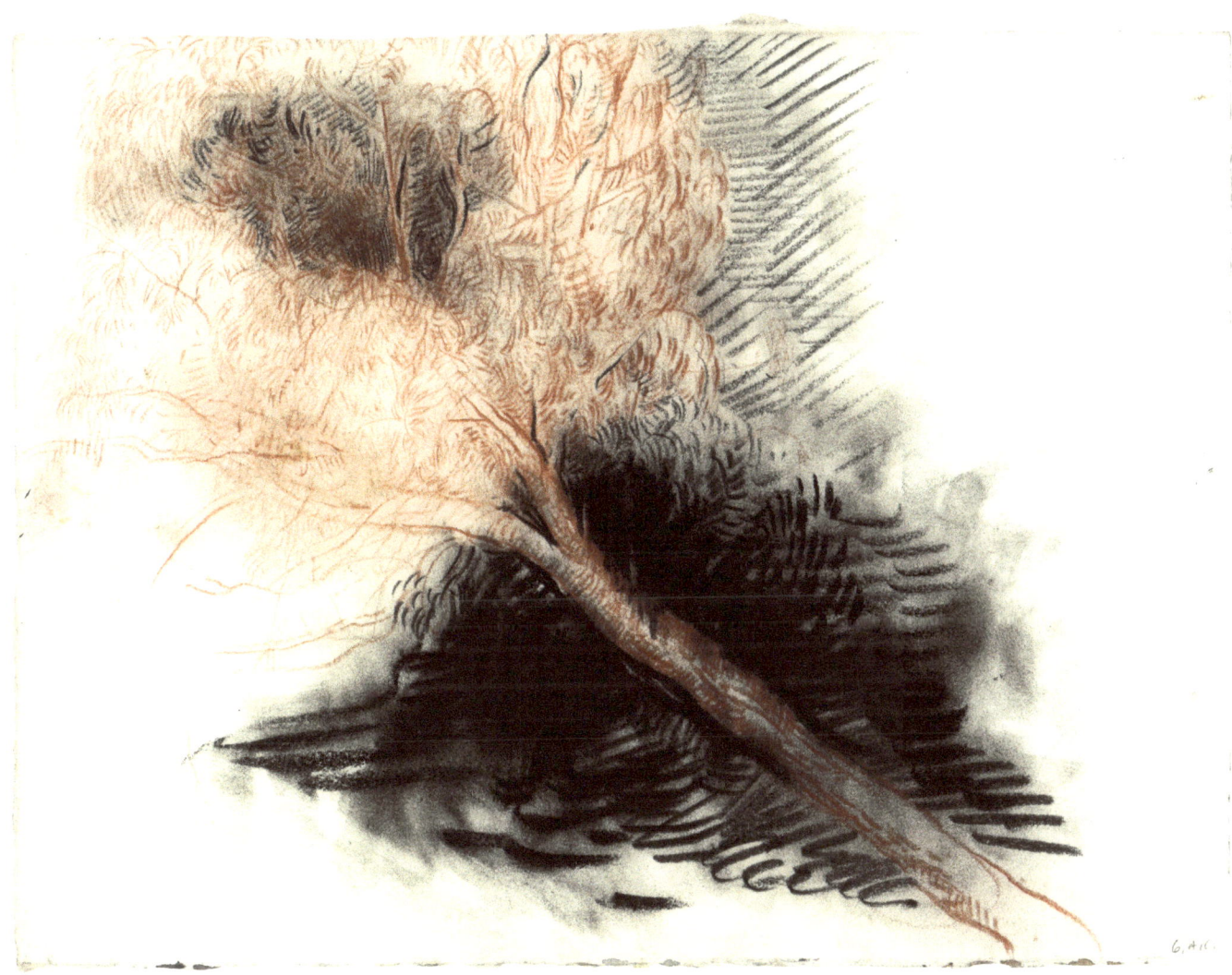

Ancient Garden, 2001, Ink on Paper, 11 x 13 inches

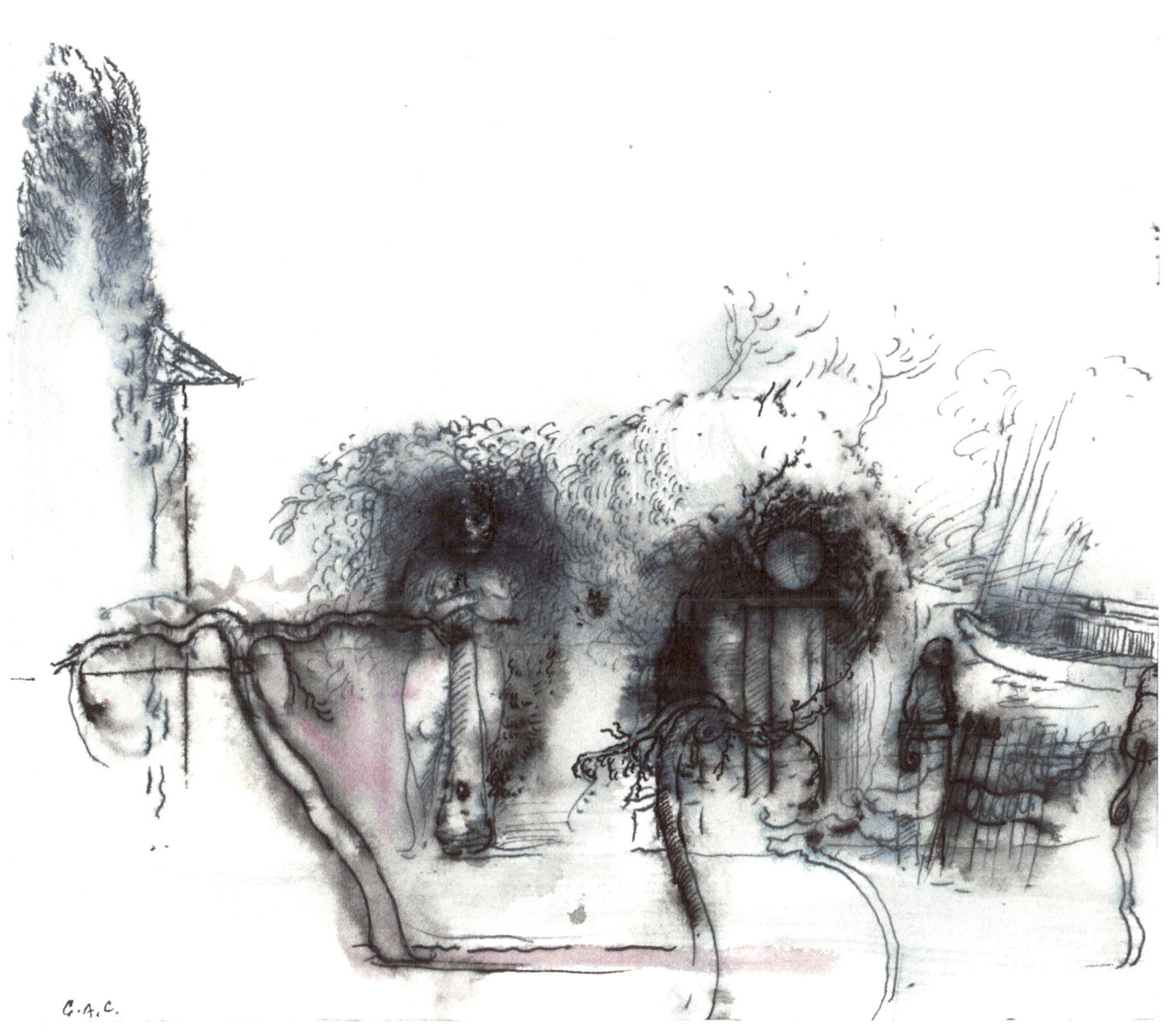

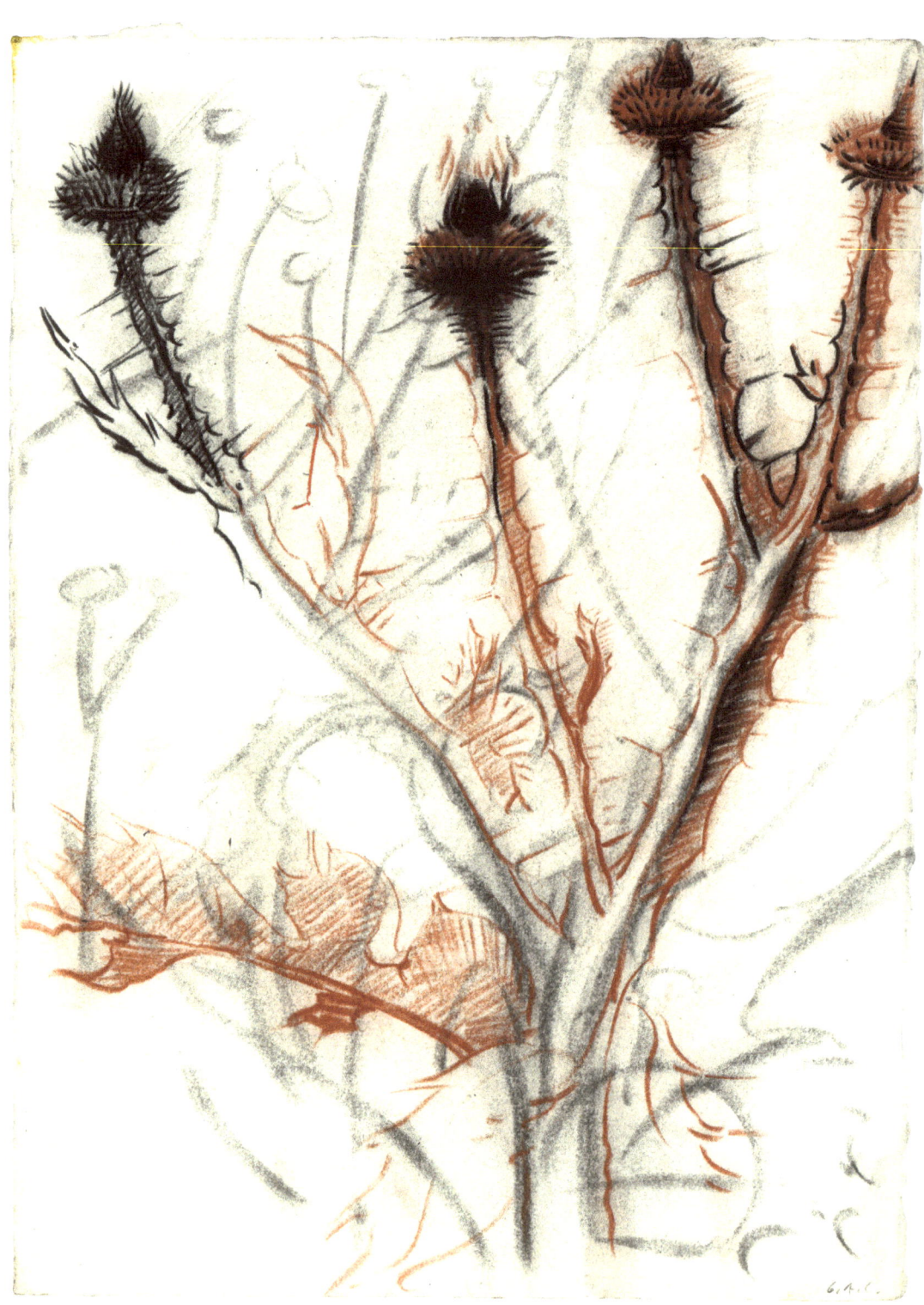

Energy Fields

In the beginning, there are dark allées, disconcerting penumbra and a branching thistle. A country estate has gone to seed; the gardener is hyper and distracted, the orchardist, a madman and visionary. Here, a tree is a fantastic sanguine candelabrum, and a sunflower, to which Redon would have tipped his hat, doubles as Cyclops. Elsewhere, a figure with large club stands guard at a gate and zephyrs agitate the skies.

These drawings are the marvelous foundation for Gregory Crane's spirited sensibility. With charcoal, conté crayon, graphite, pen and ink, and a bit of wash, he begins the journey toward the canvas, deploying a mix of swift crosshatchings, architectural calculations and acrobatic lines. These fields of energy are carried forth into those landscapes that have been captivating us for decades.

What art historian Alexander Eliot wrote about Charles Burchfield is applicable to the artist at hand. It was Burchfield's view of nature "as experience, and not just a setting," Eliot wrote, that distinguished him "from the more polite landscape painters of Europe and their American followers." Crane's drawings underscore his place in this unconventional lineage even as they offer evidence of the care he takes in developing his pictorial ideas.

Through these drawings, the artist invites us to explore new corners of his imagination. In the beginning, there is a cardamom bud and a potting shed, twisting foliage and capricious winds—the world according to Gregory Crane.

Carl Little, 2009

Thistle Plant, 1995, Charcoal, Conte Crayon and Pencil on Paper, 15 x 11 inches

Stowe Valley Vermont (The End As A Student), 1979, Pencil on Paper, 13 x 20 inches

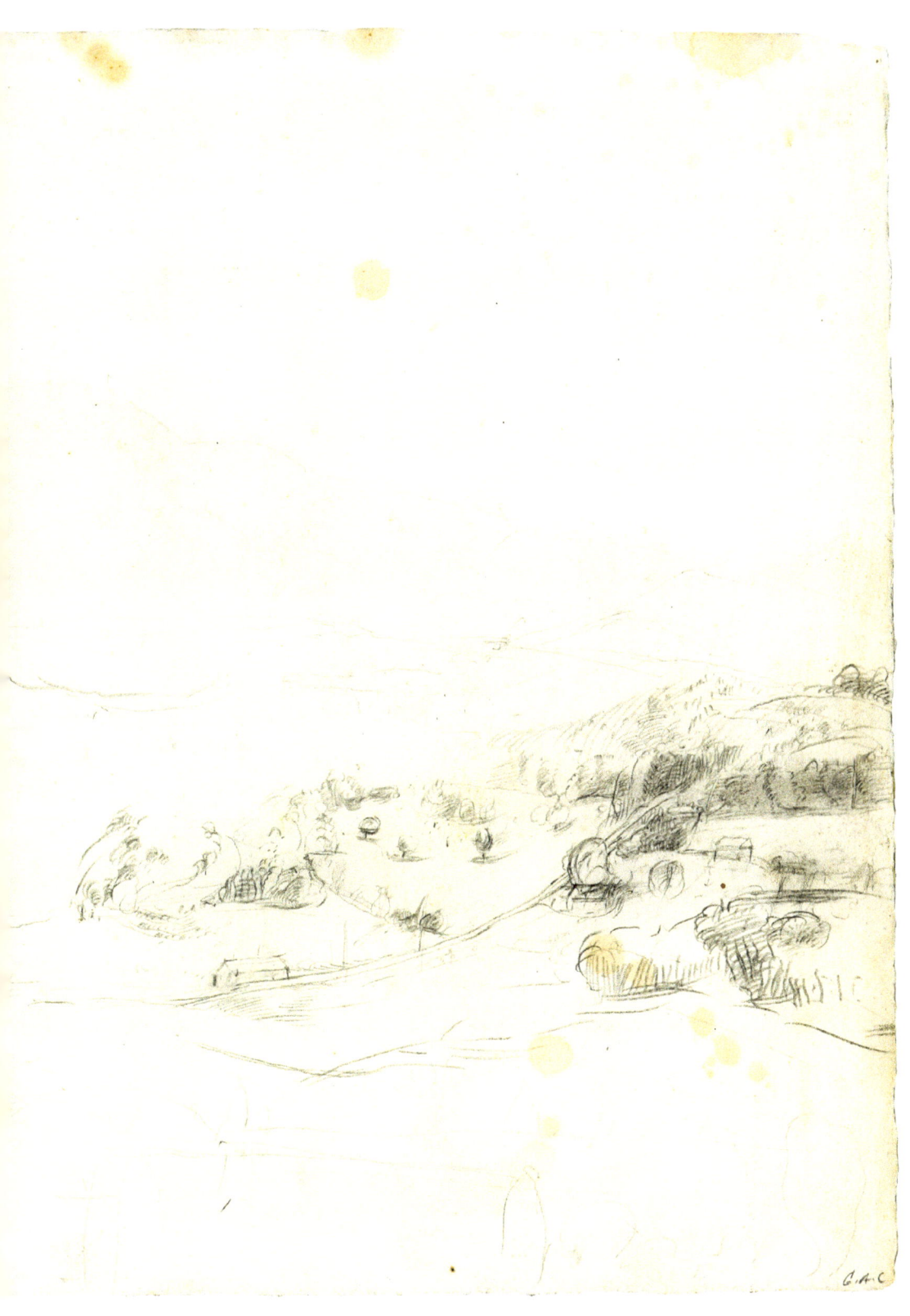

Prairie w/Cloud, 2008, Ink, Pencil and Conte Crayon on Paper, 15 x 11 inches

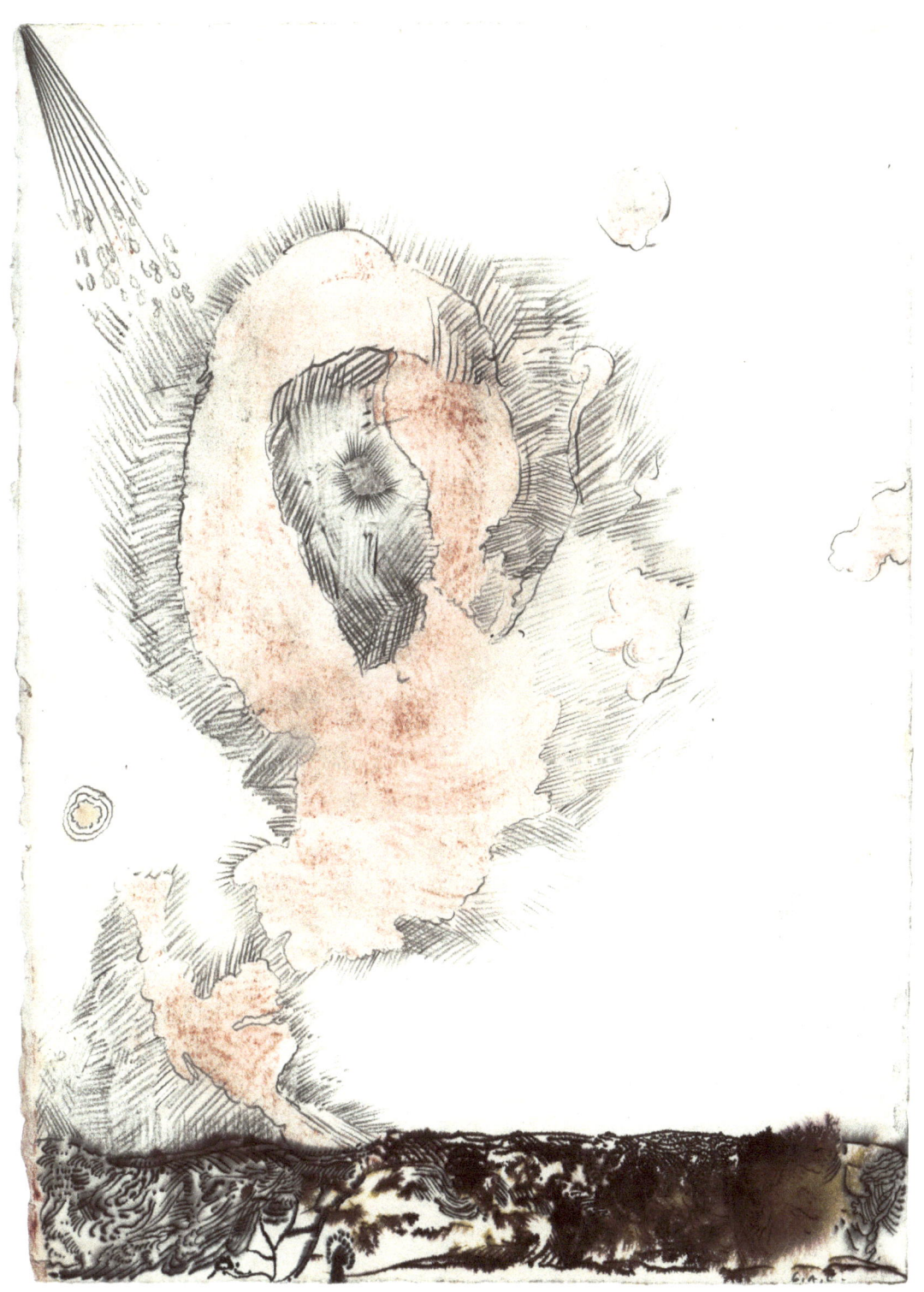

1979 - 1989

Jewel's Sunflower, 1982, Ink on Paper, 15 x 11 inches

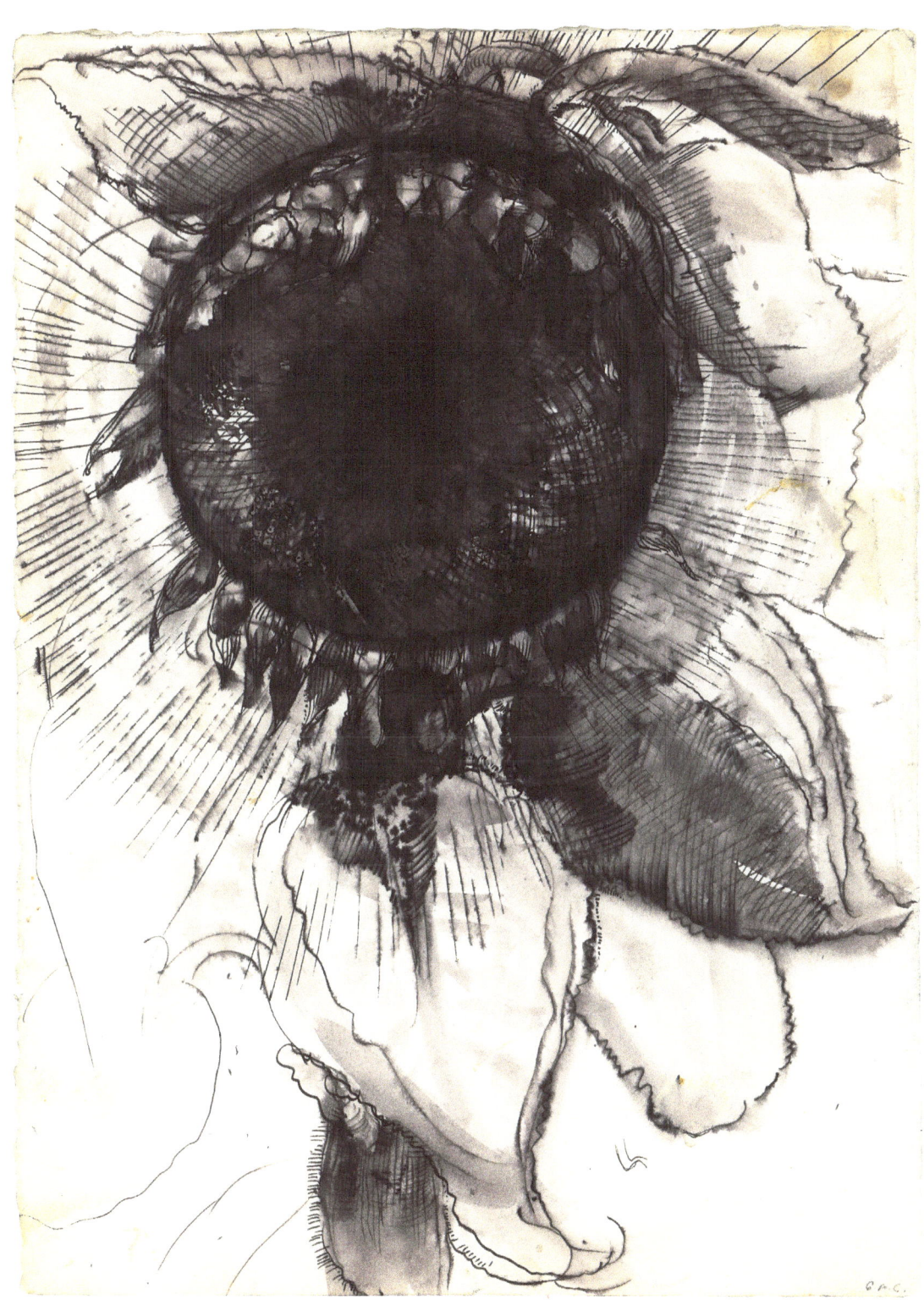

Hill – So. Vermont (working drawing), 1984, Charcoal, Conte Crayon, Ink and Pencil on Paper, 11 x 15 inches

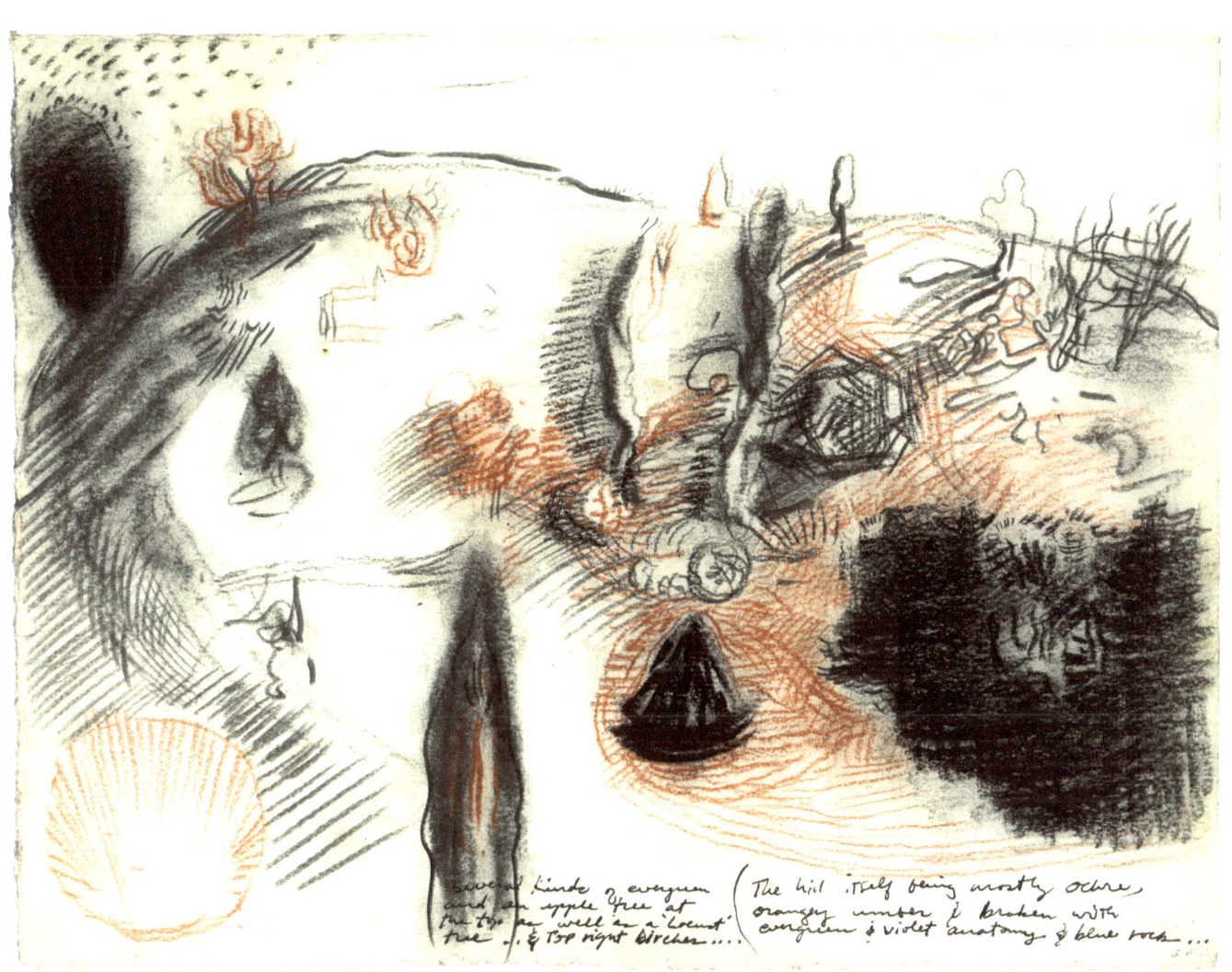

several kinds of evergreen
and an apple tree at
the top as well as a 'locust'
tree ... & top right birches ....

(The hill itself being mostly ochre,
orangey umber & broken with
evergreen & violet anatomy & blue rock ...

Cornfield Near Hill Top (So. Vermont), 1983, Charcoal, Conte Crayon and Pencil on Paper, 11 x 15 inches

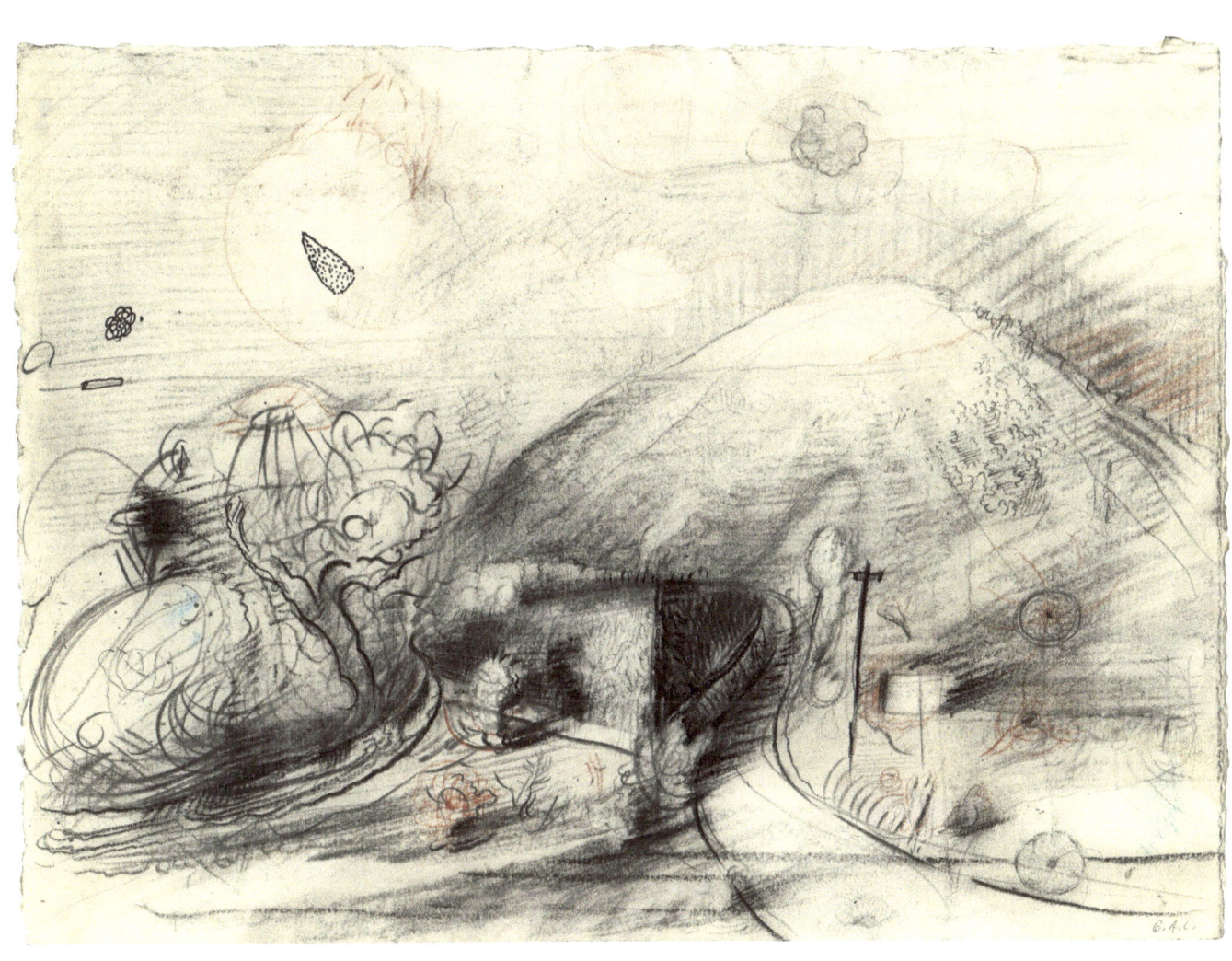

Looking At The Night Sky, 1985, Charcoal and Pencil on Paper, 11 x 15 inches

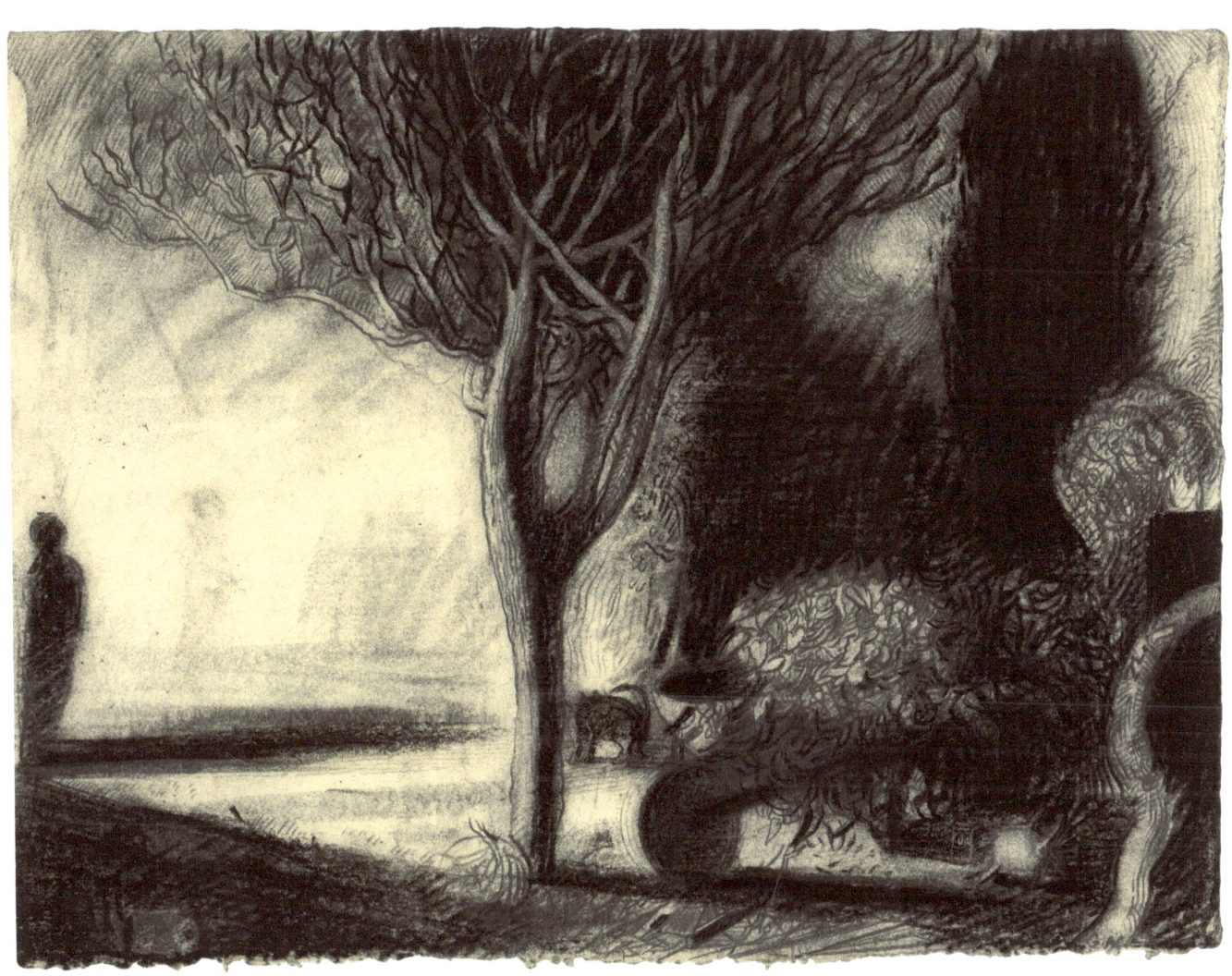

Trees w/ Cat, 1989, Ink on Paper, 11 x 15 inches

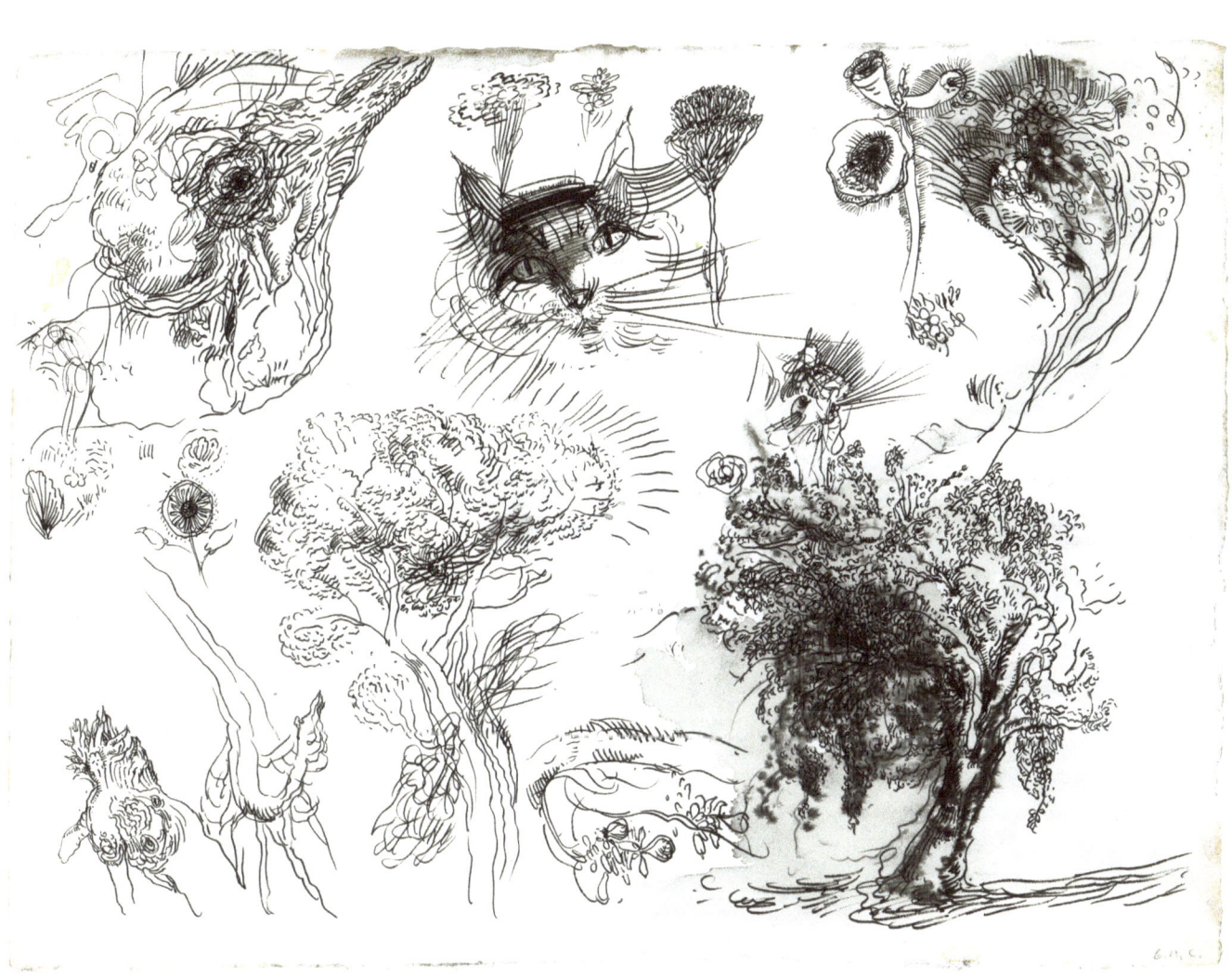

Tree Study (Madrona), 1986 – 1987, Charcoal and Conte Crayon on Paper, 15 x 11 inches

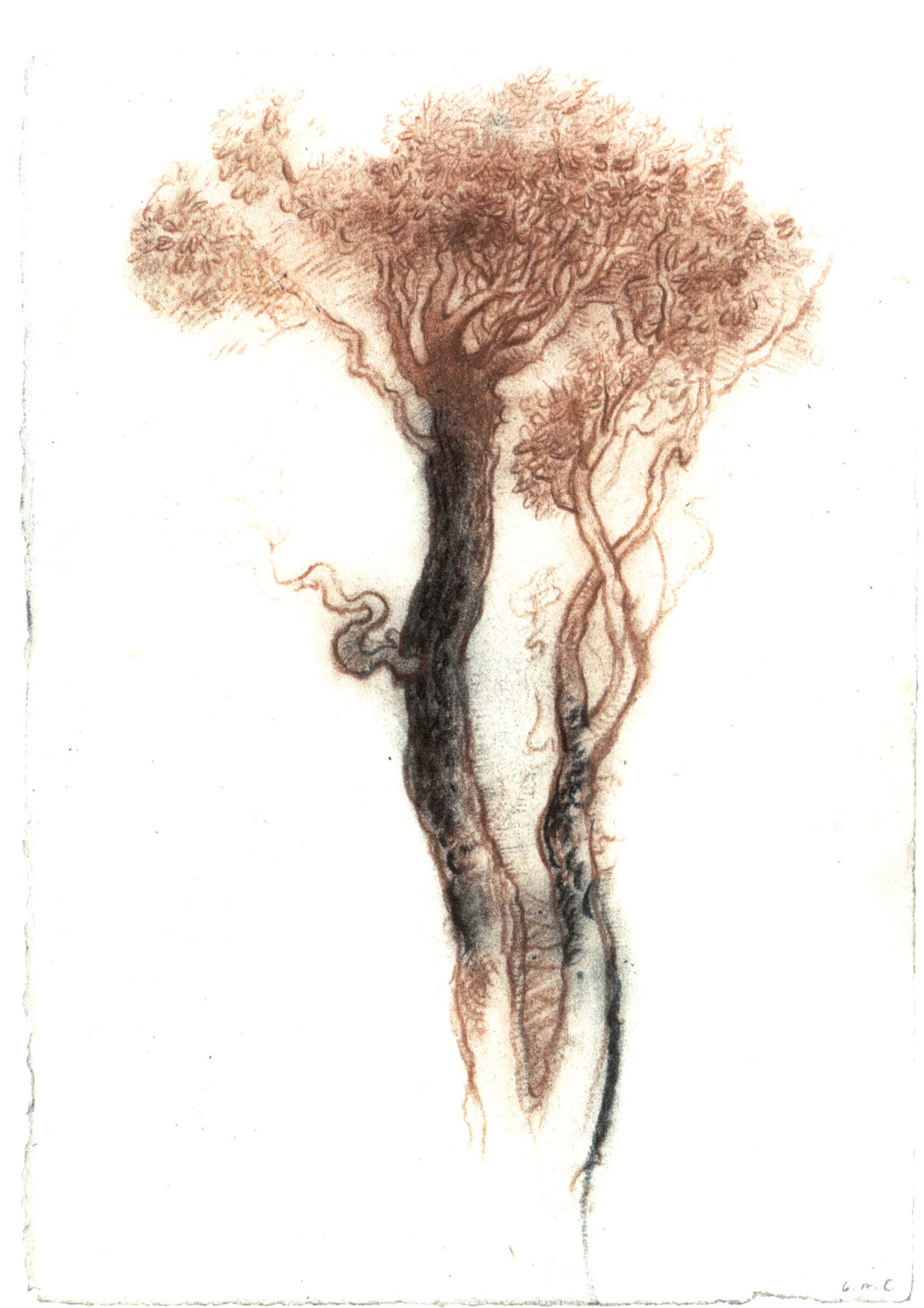

Tree Study, 1986 – 1987, Conte Crayon on Paper, 15 x 11 inches

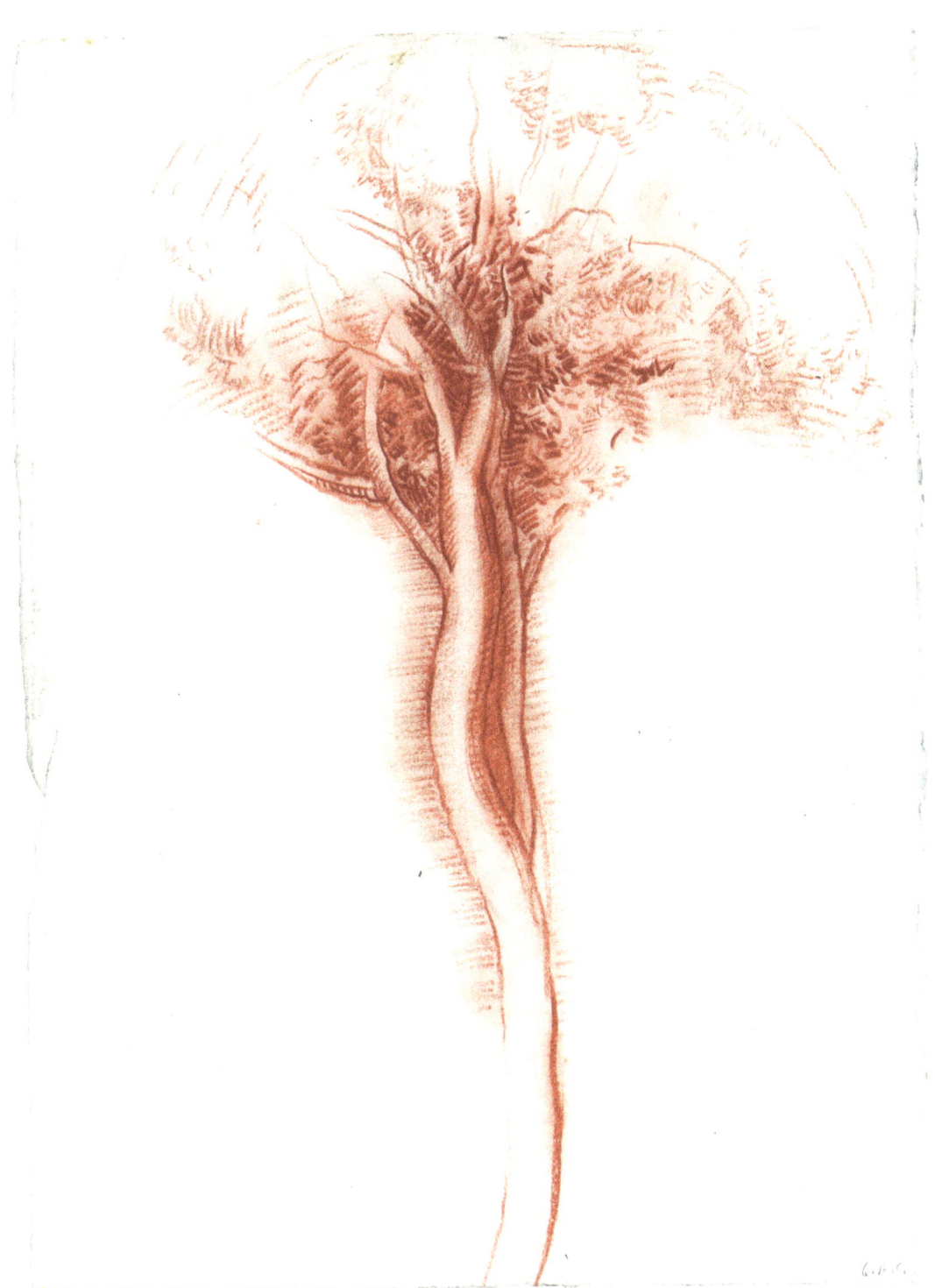

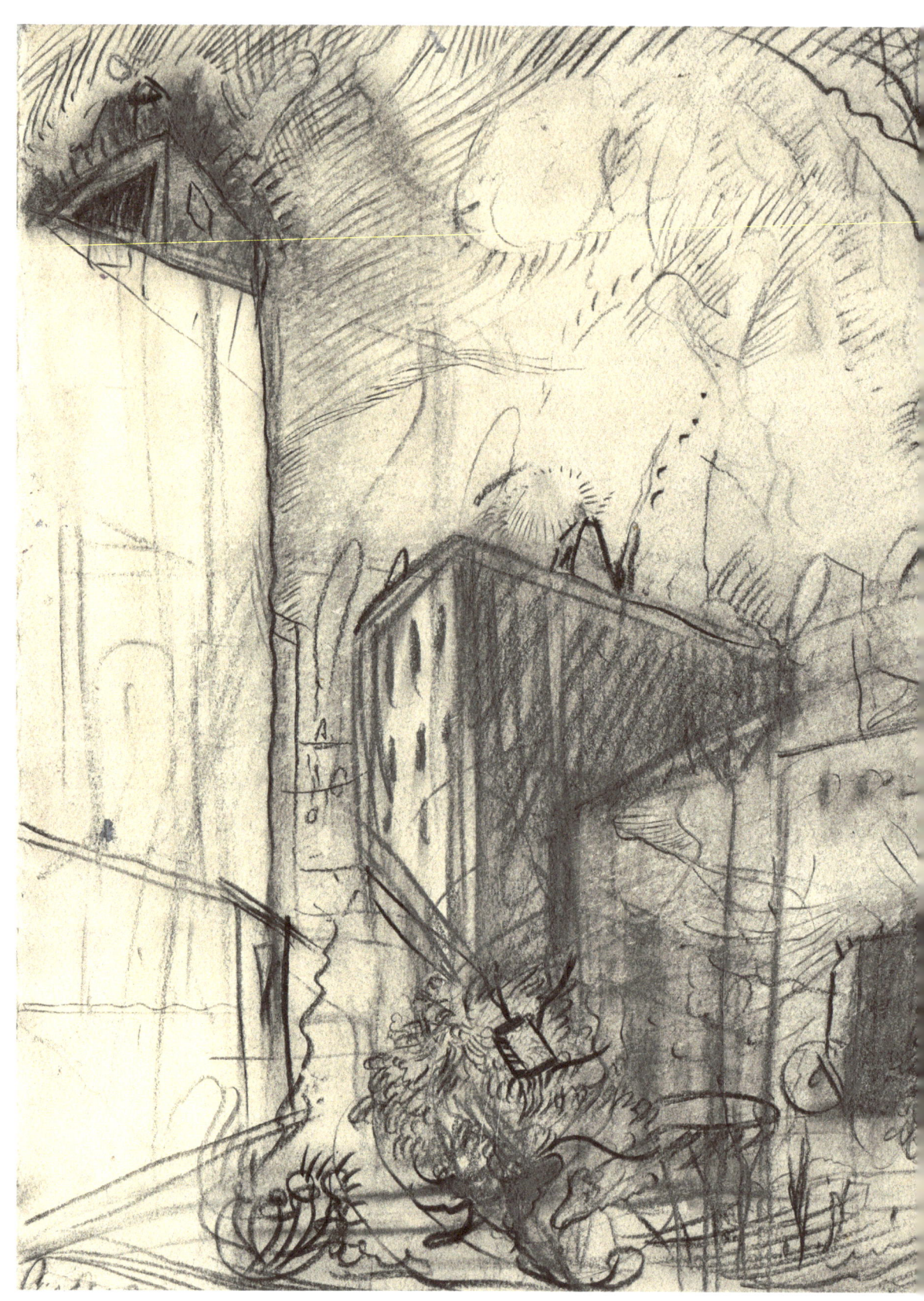

Study for the Winter Pools, 1985, Pencil on Paper, 12.5 x 19 inches

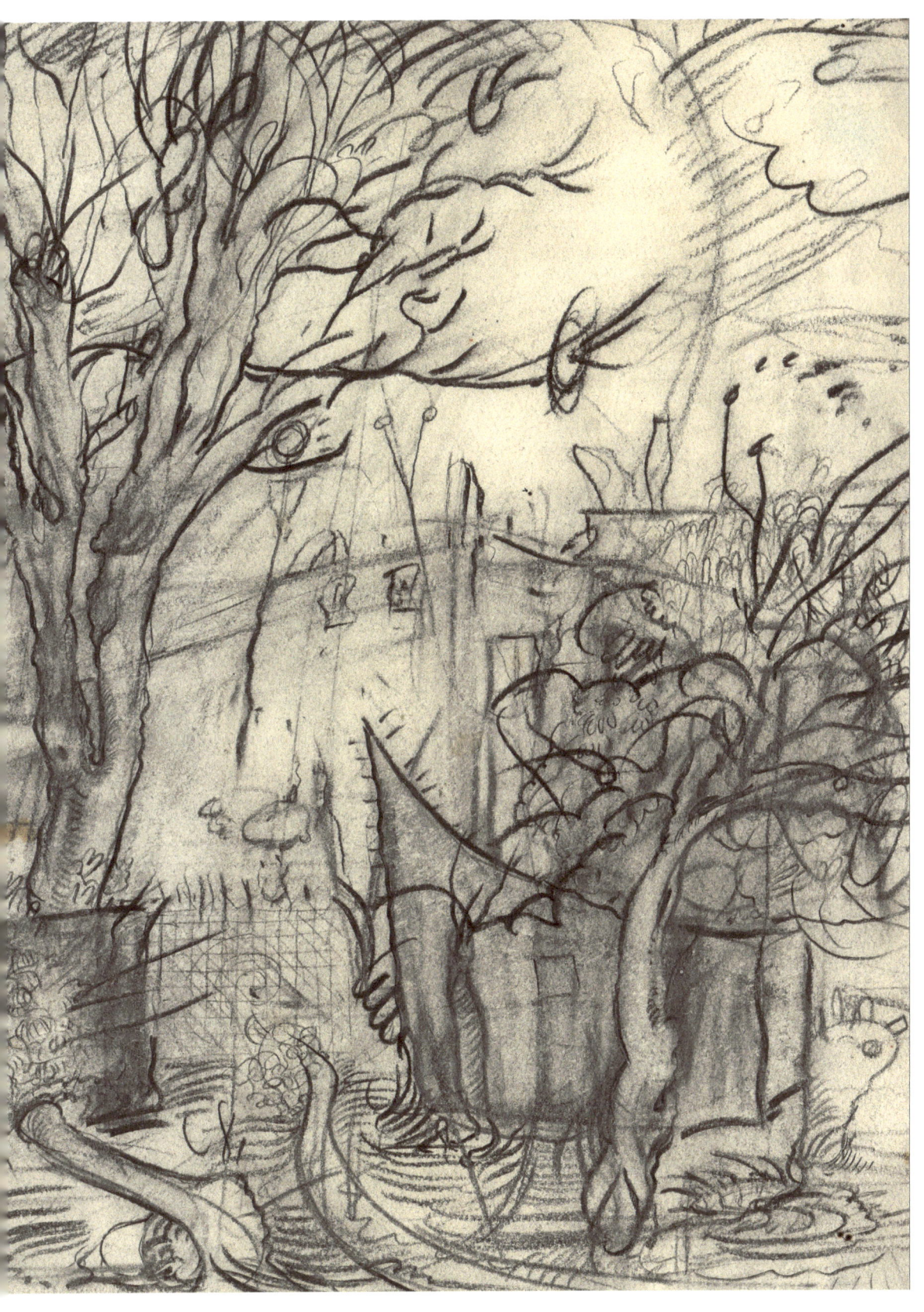

Hydrangea & Climatis, 1988 – 1989, Pencil on Paper, 11 x 15 inches

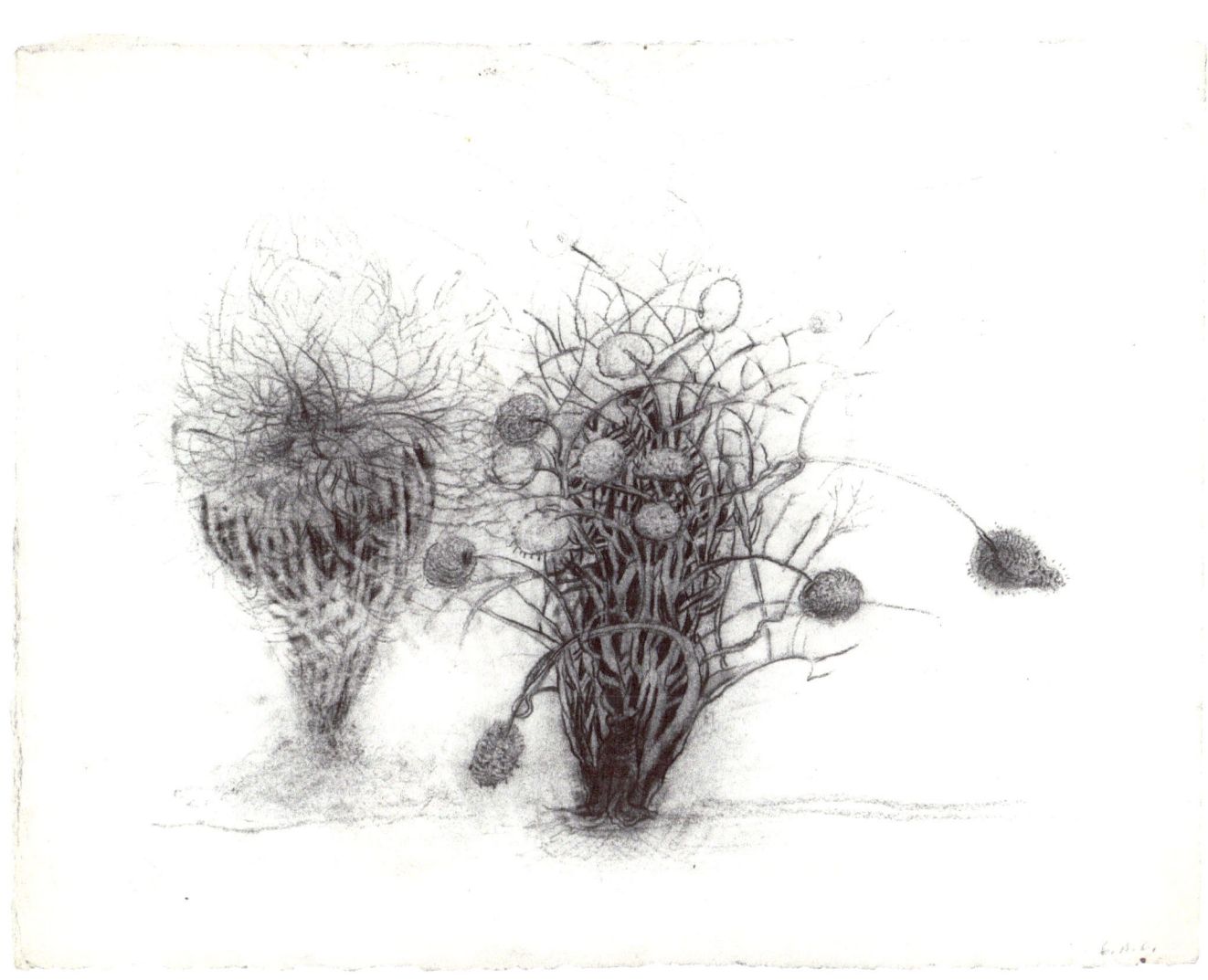

Moonlight w/Axe, 1983, Charcoal, Chalk and Pencil on Paper, 12 x 17.5 inches

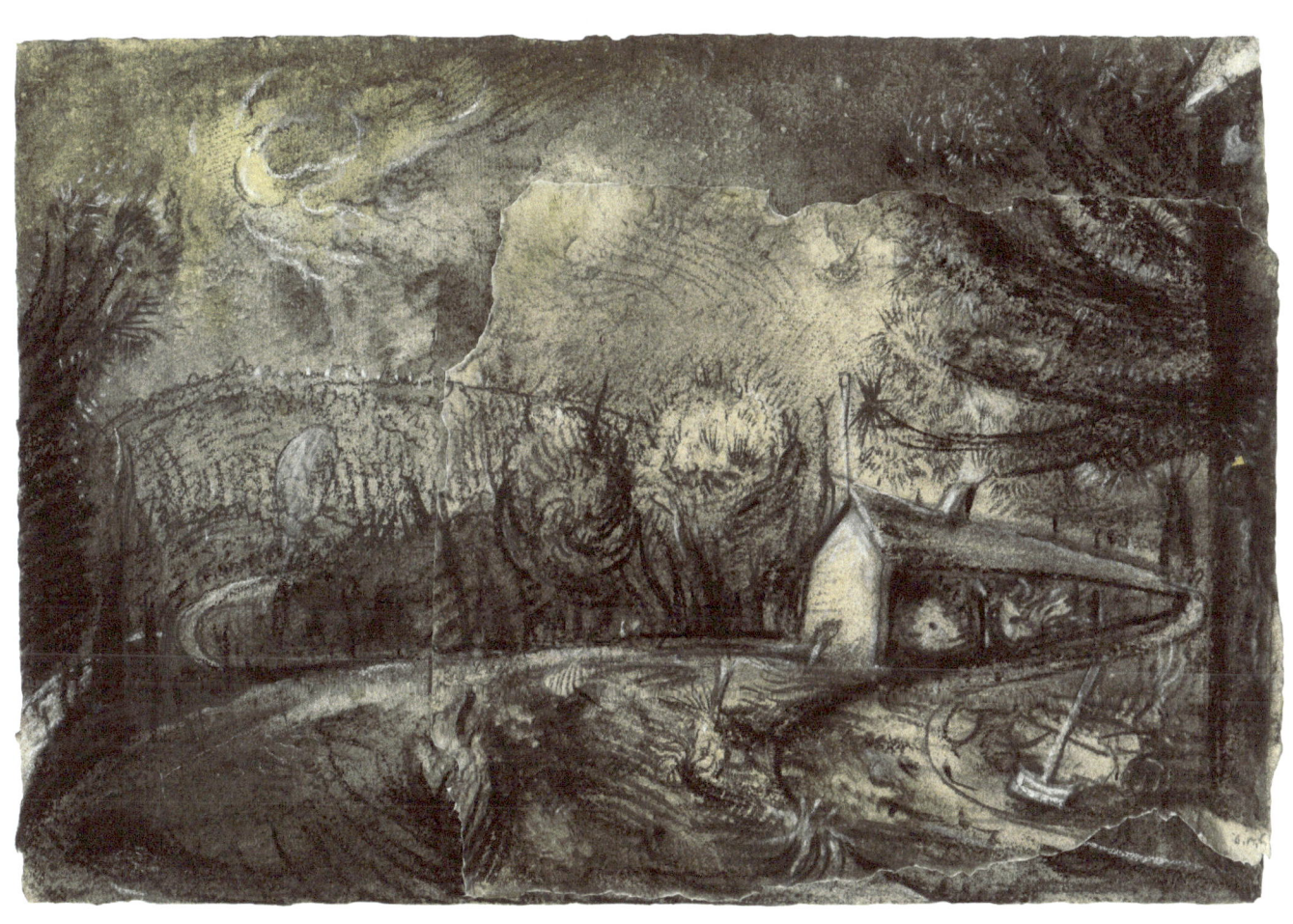

So. Vermont Hillside, 1985, Charcoal, Conte Crayon and Pencil on Paper, 11 x 15 inches

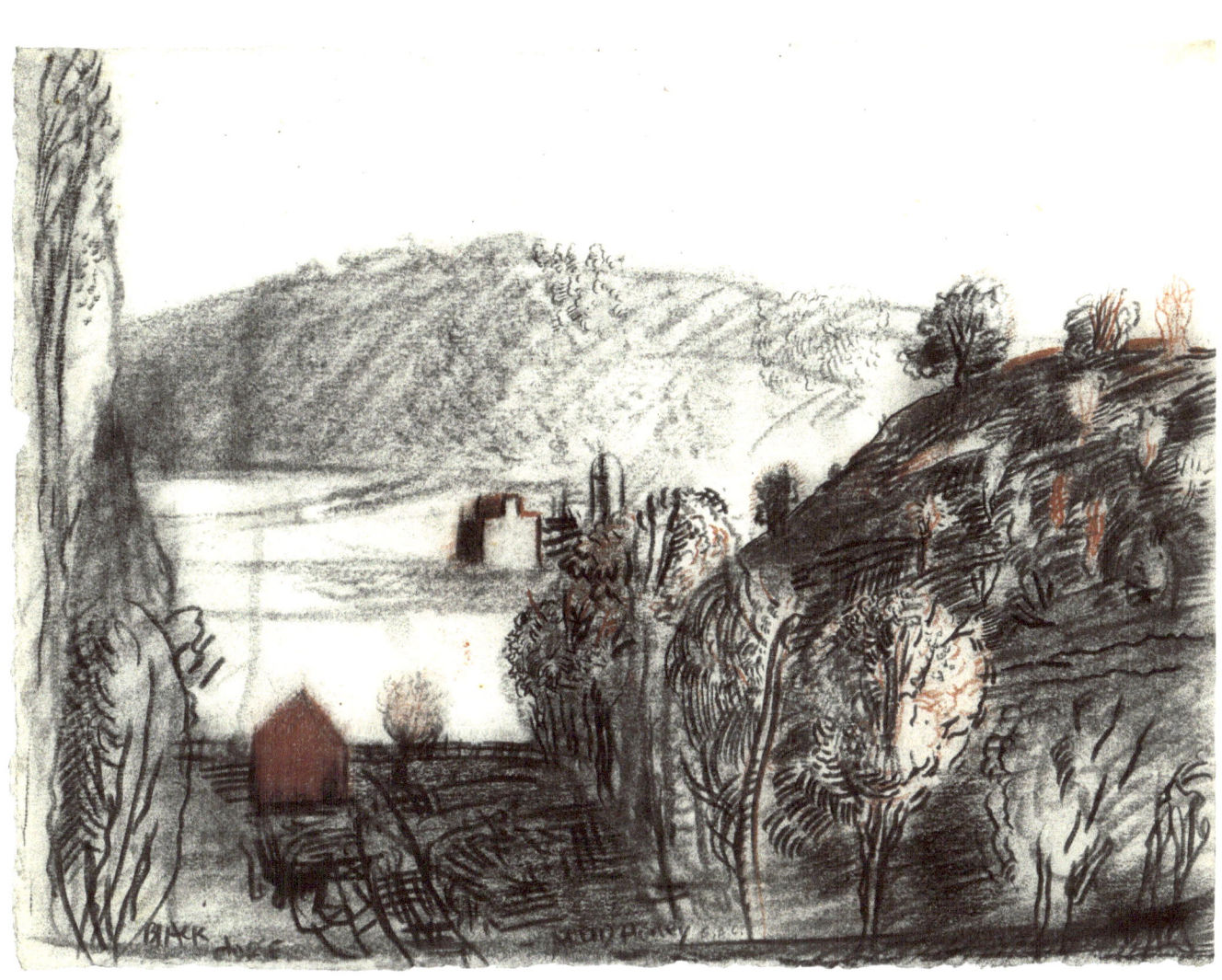

1990 - 1999

Italian Studies, 1998, Ink on Paper, 15 x 11 inches

Giovani Antonio Bazzi

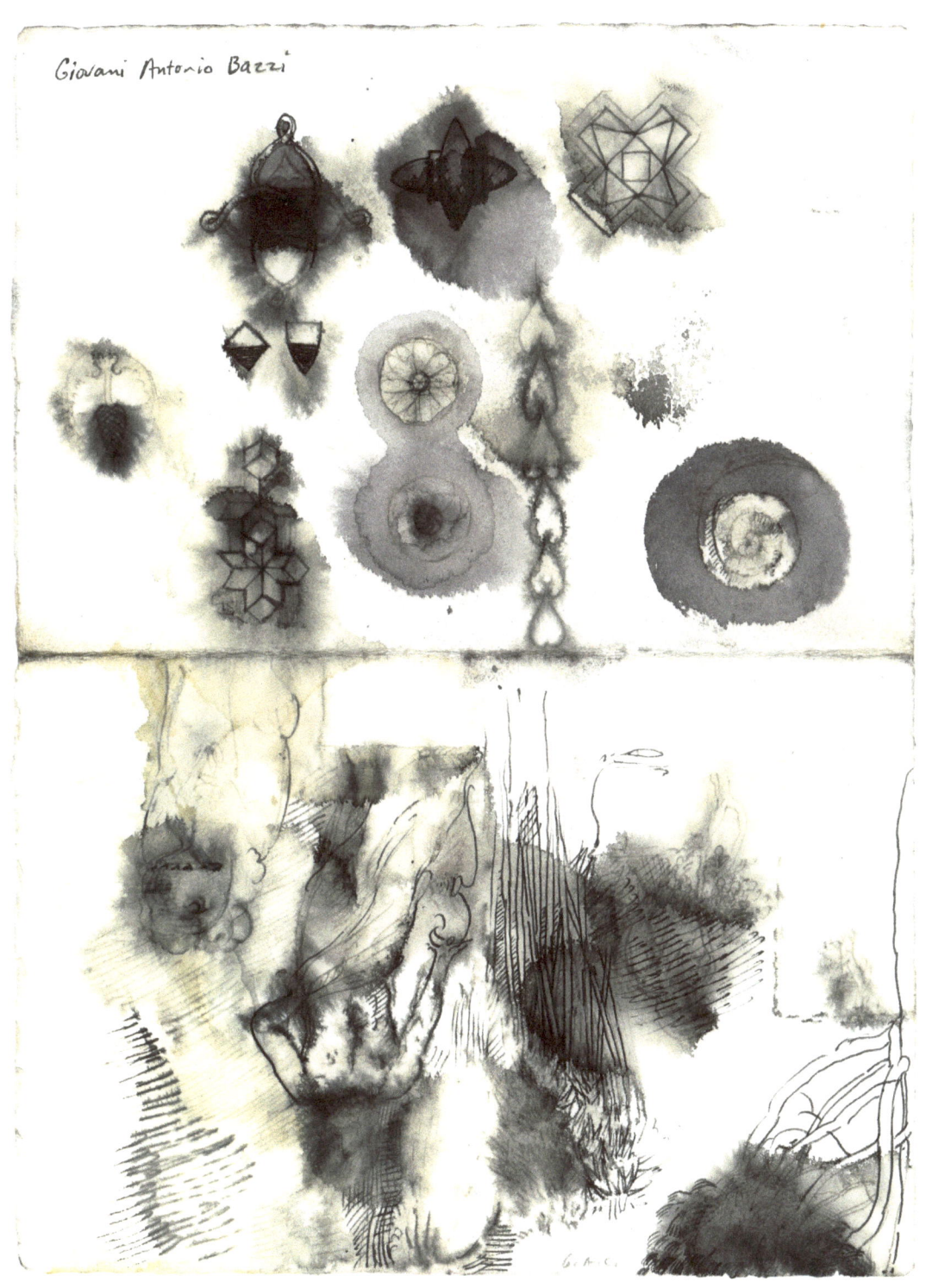

Spring Study of June's Garden, 1995, Charcoal, Conte Crayon and Ink on Paper, 11 x 15 inches

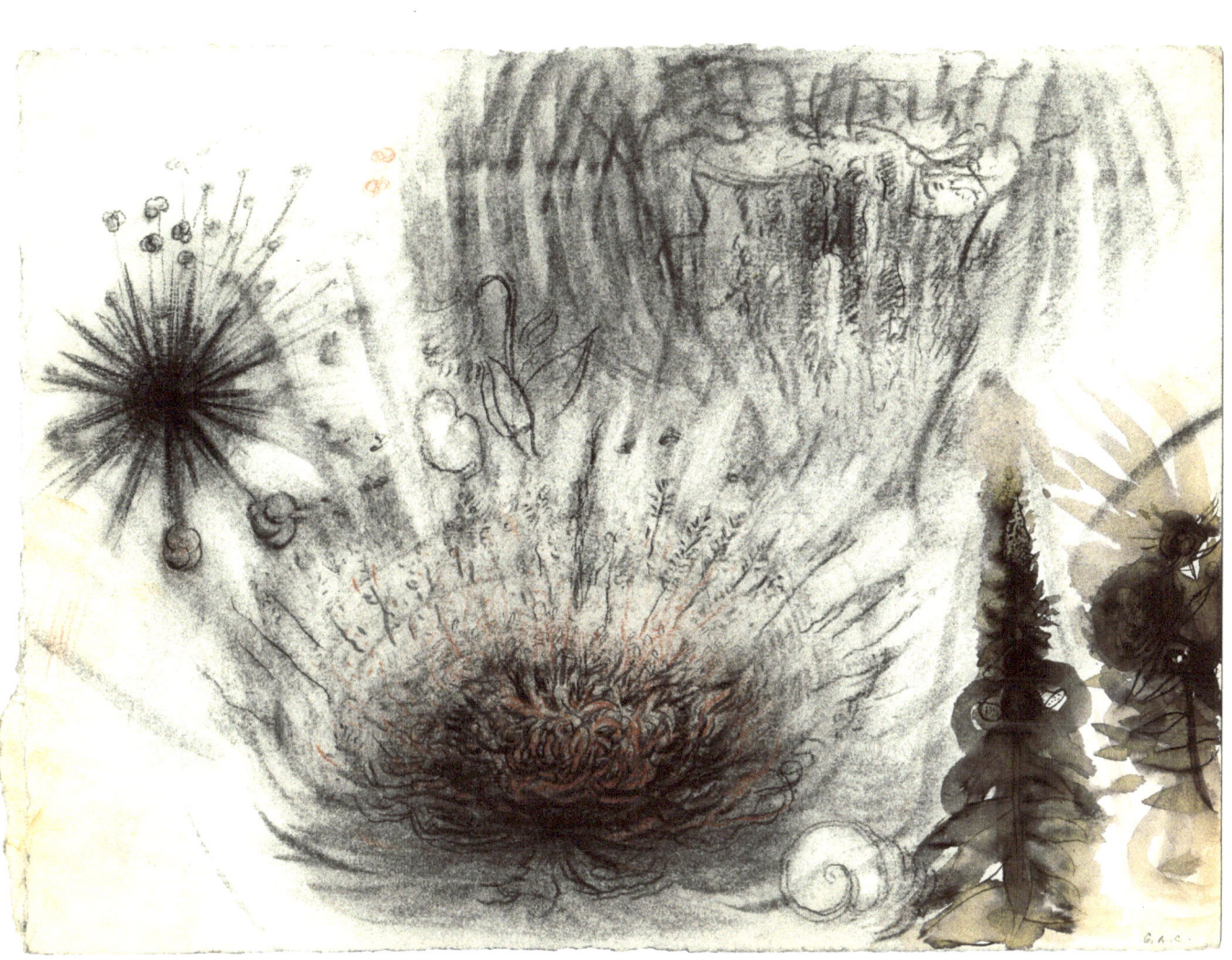

Wheel Barrow w/Blimp, 1997, Charcoal, Conte Crayon and Pencil on Paper, 11 x 15 inches

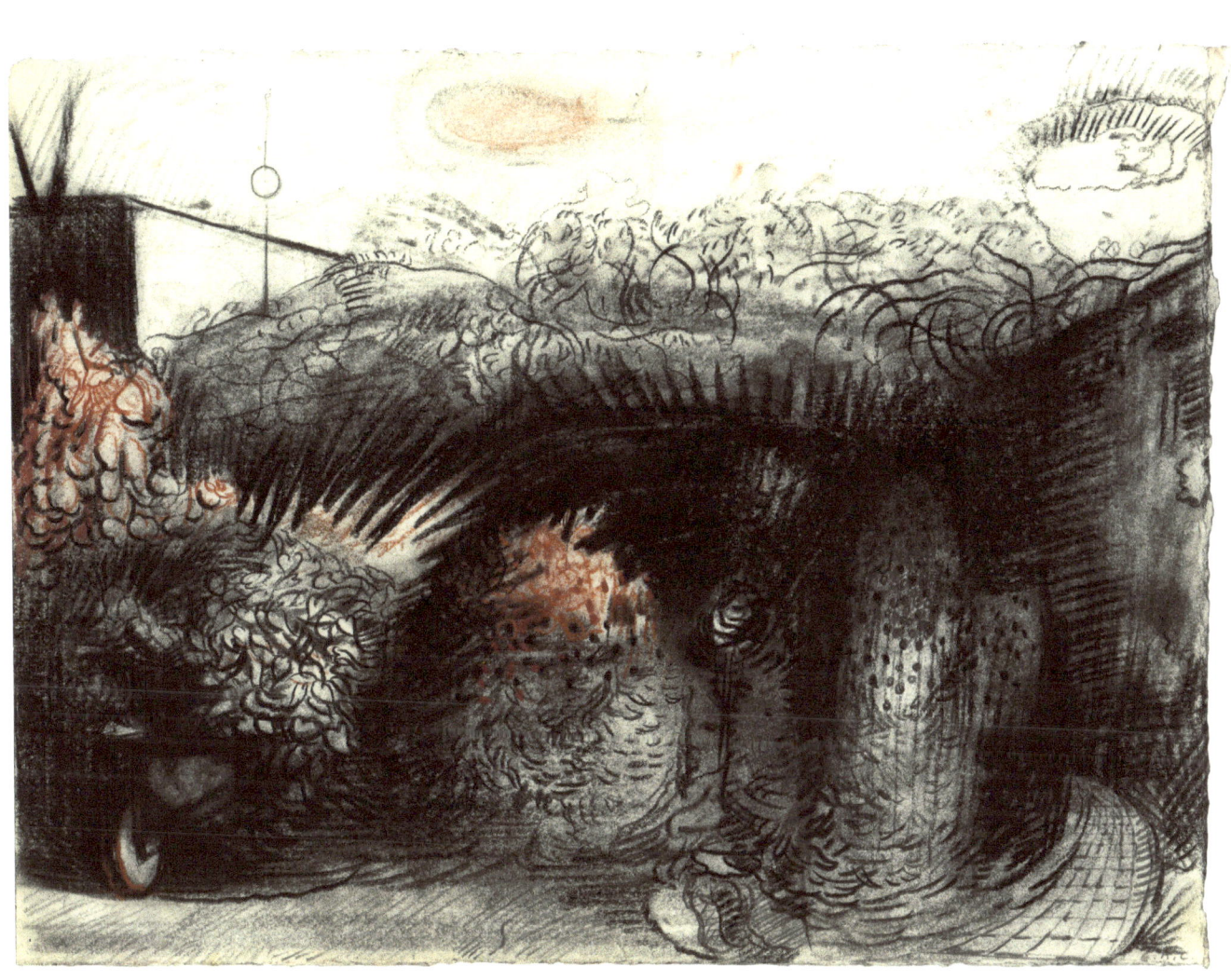

Mike & Anne's Garden, 1991, Ink on Paper, 11 x 15 inches

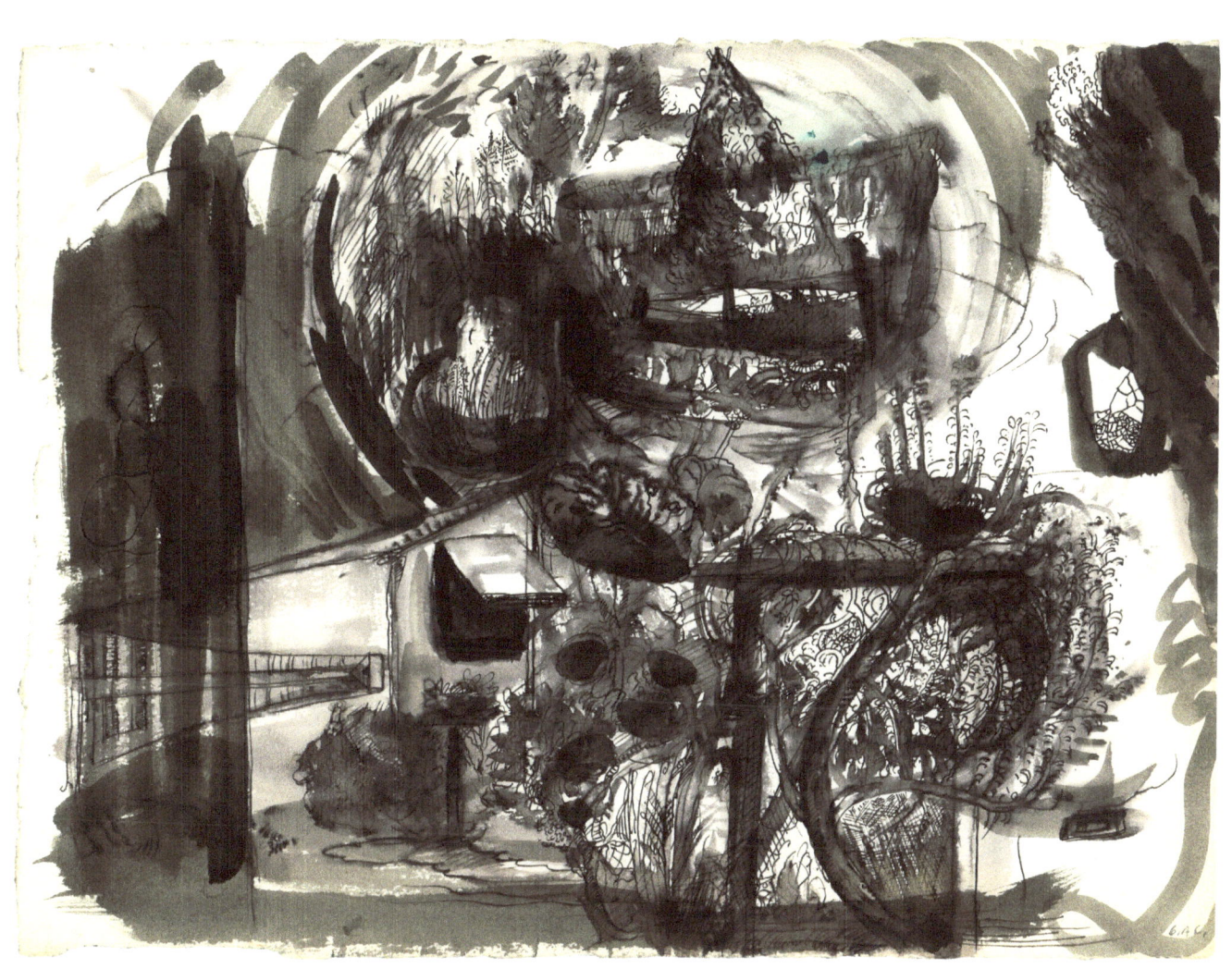

Yucca (Little Studio), 1991 – 1992, Ink on Paper, 15 x 11 inches

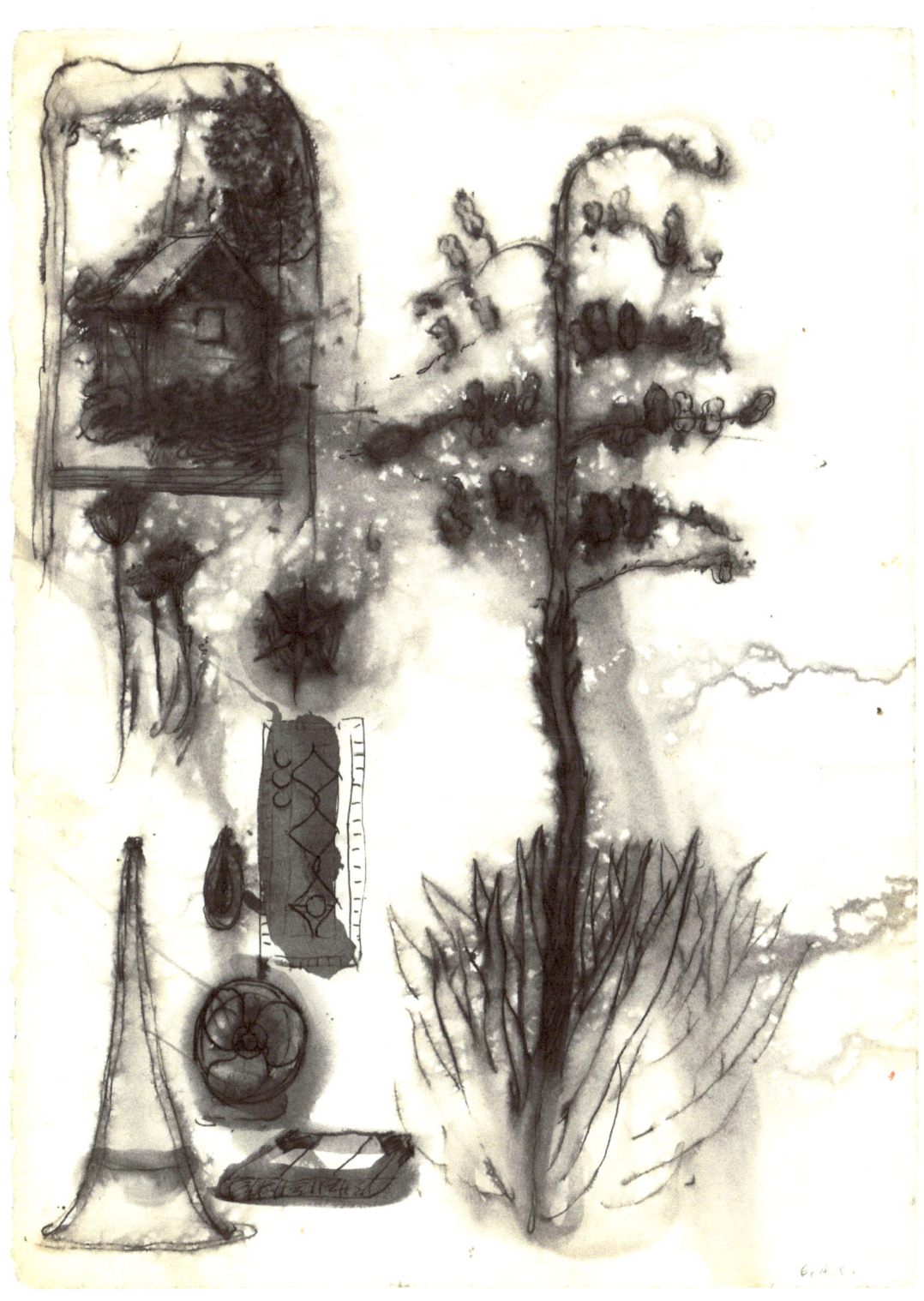

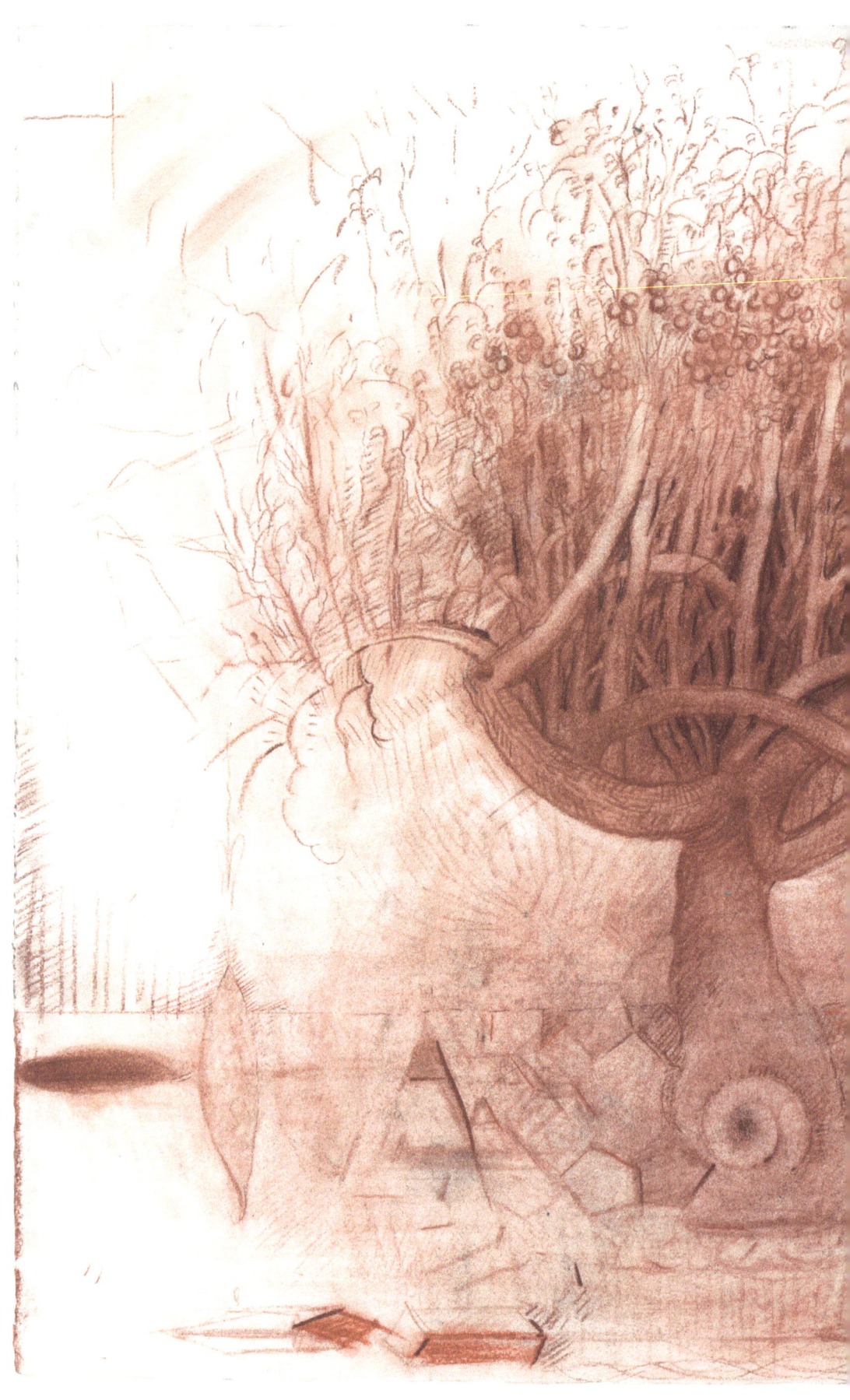

Ripe Apple with View of Underground, 1991-2, Chalk and Conte Crayon on Paper, 22 x 30 inches

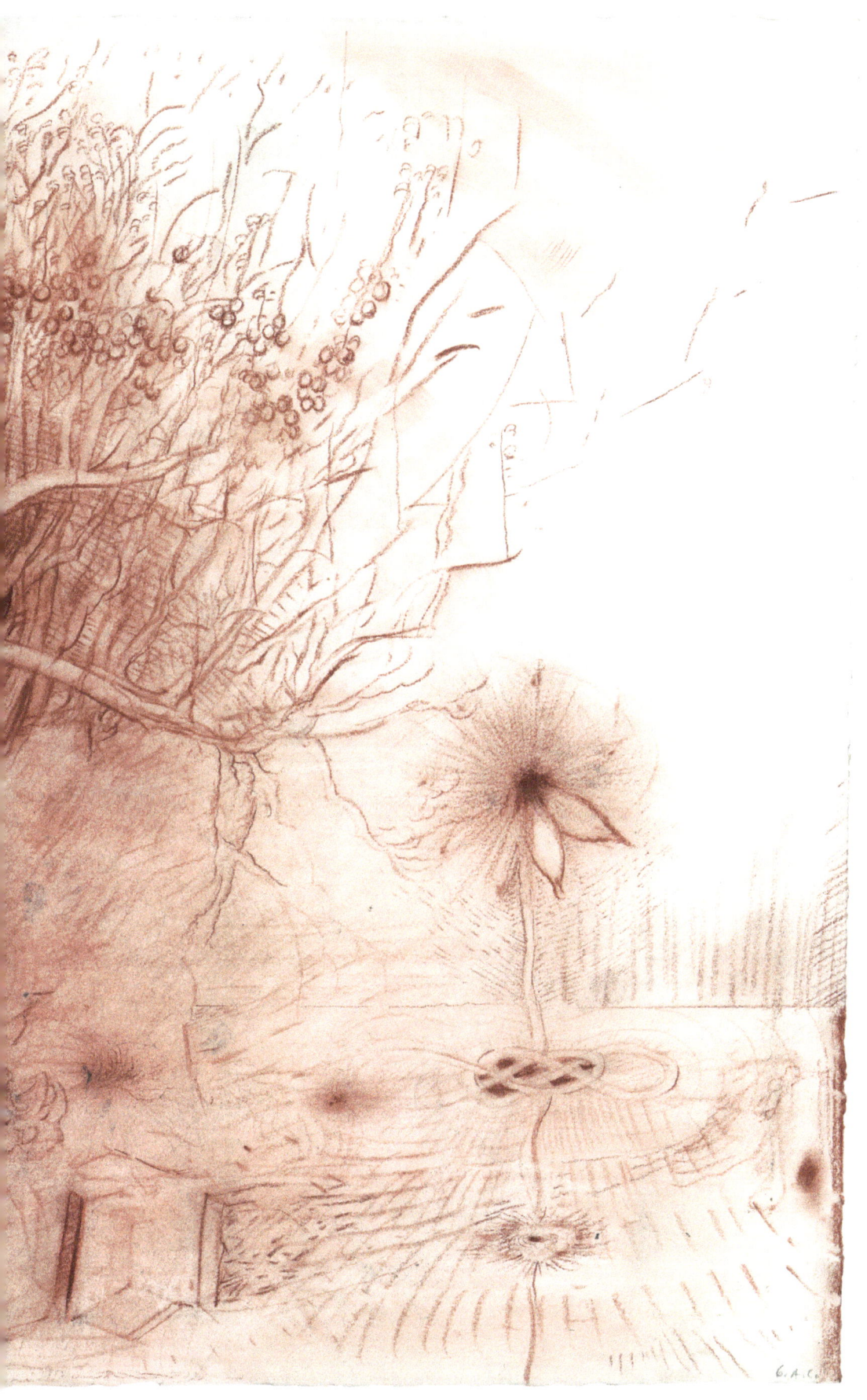

Squash Studies, 1990, Charcoal, Conte Crayon and Pencil on Paper, 11 x 15 inches

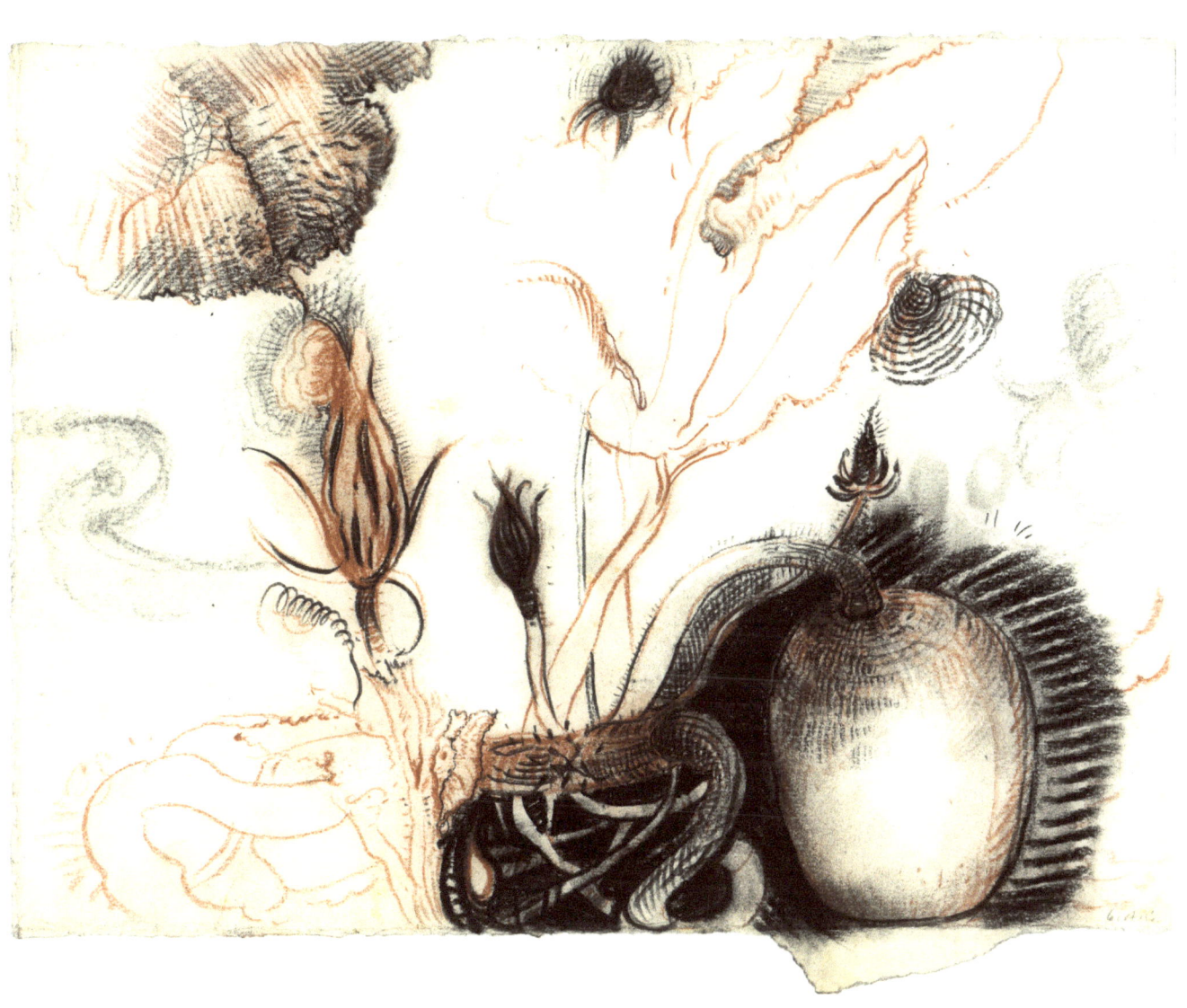

Man w/Abandoned Pool, 1990 – 1991, Charcoal and Pencil on Paper, 15 x 11 inches

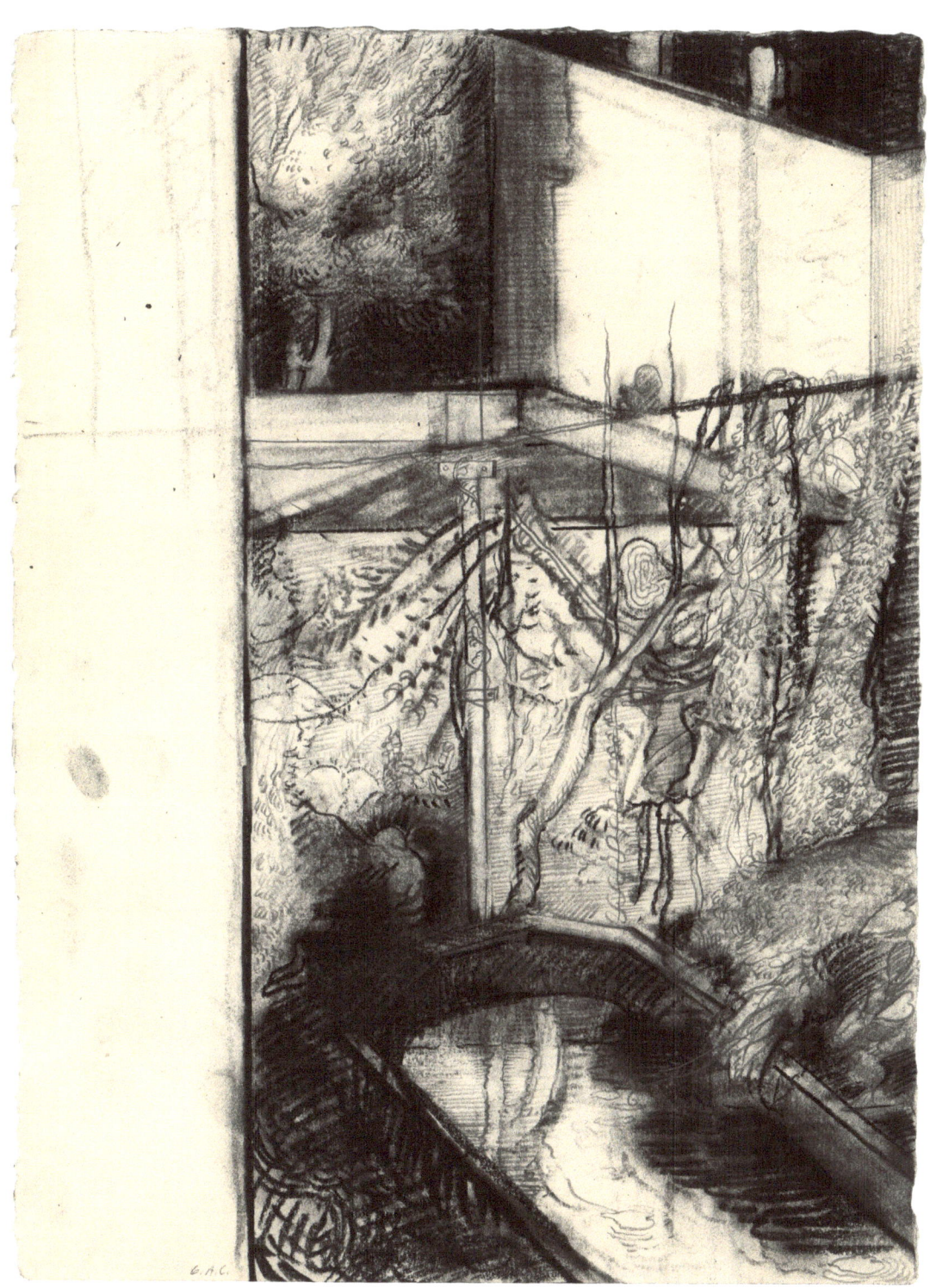

Multiple Vista Study, 1991, Ink on Paper, 15 x 11 inches

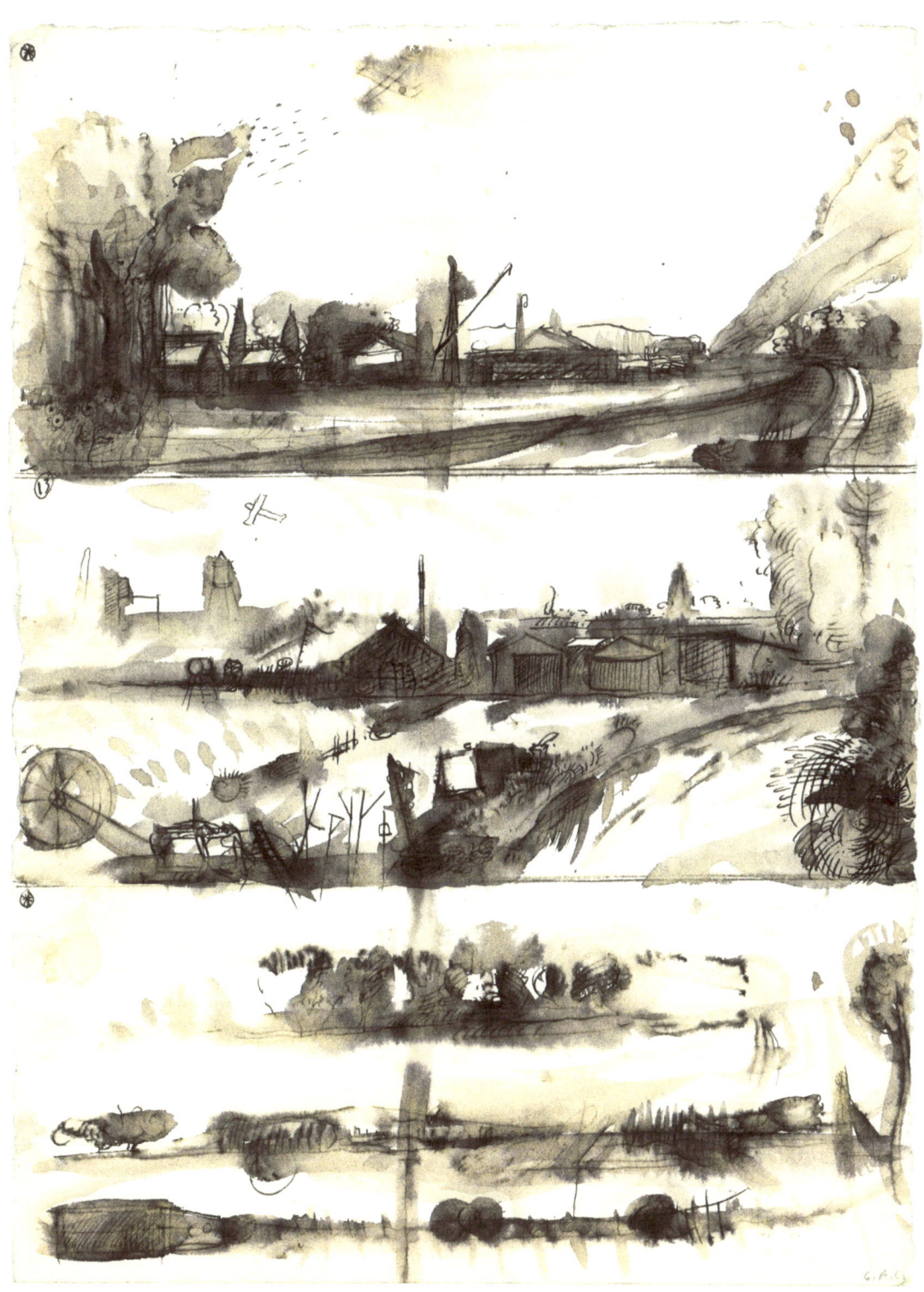

Moonlight Study, 1990, Ink on Paper, 15 x 11 inches

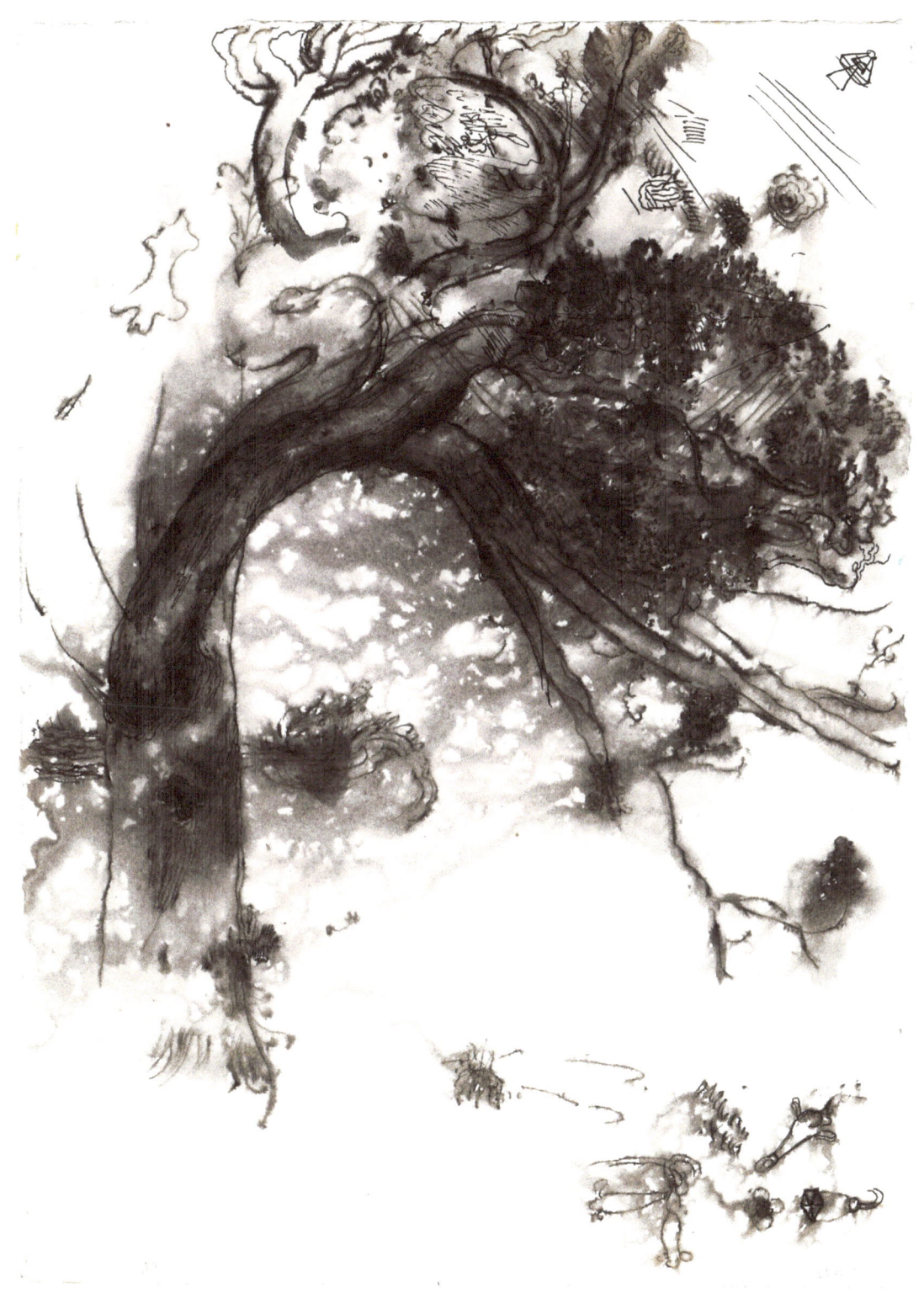

Study for Domestic Scene, 1996 – 1997, Charcoal and Pencil on Paper, 11 x 15 inches

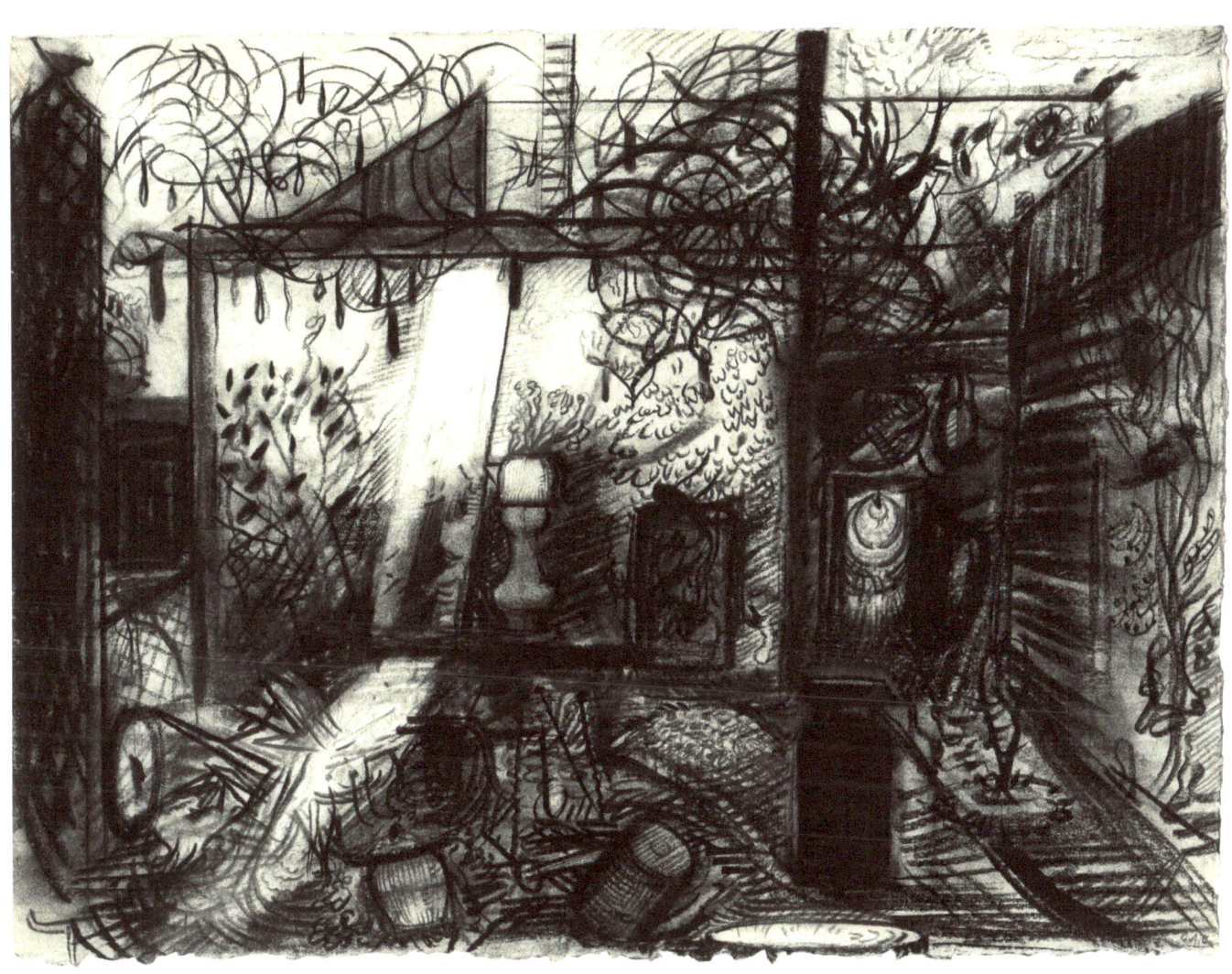

Apple w/Implements II, 1993, Charcoal, Conte Crayon and Pencil on Paper, 11 x 15 inches

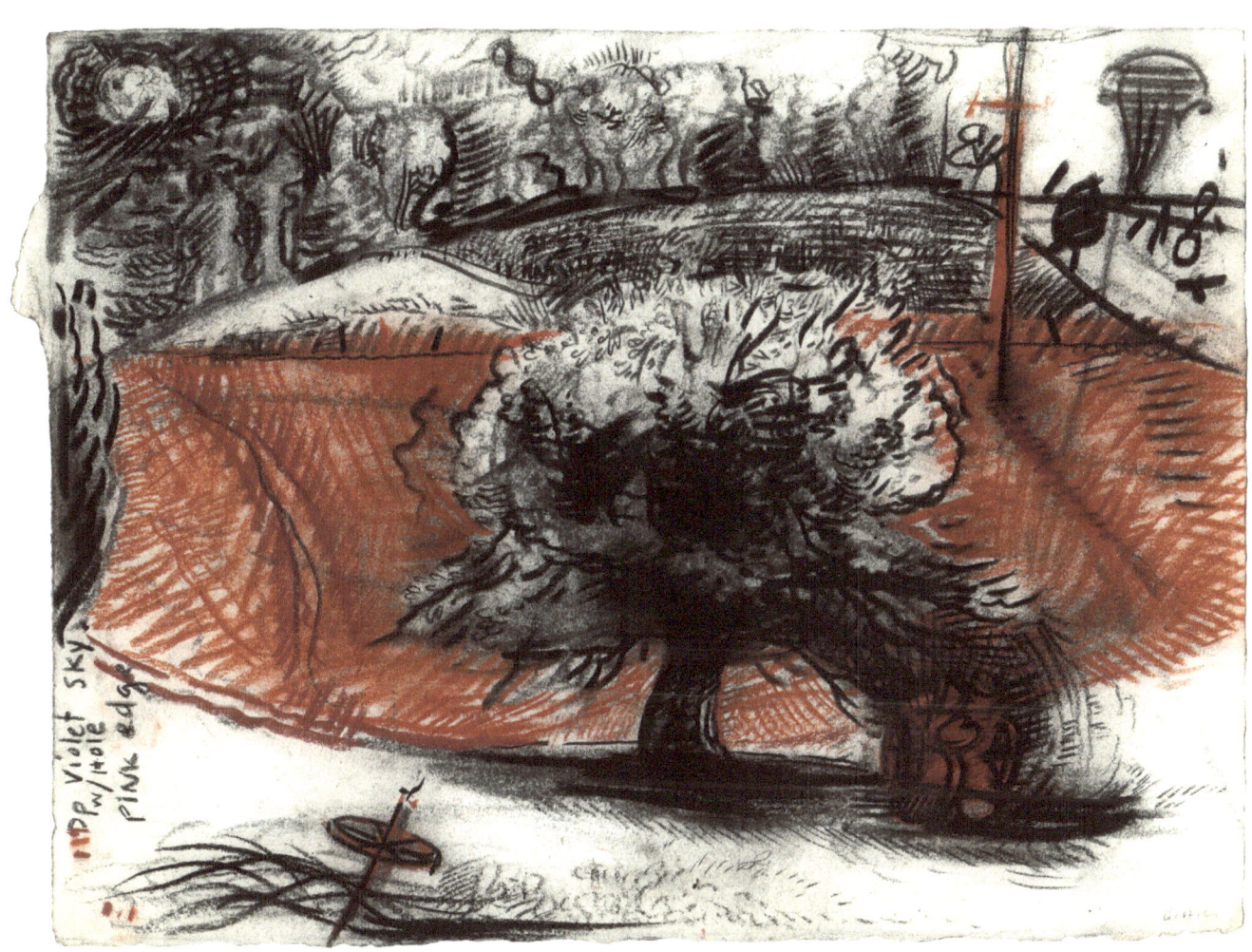

Water Tank/Cooling Tower, 1990, Ink on Paper, 10 x 13 inches

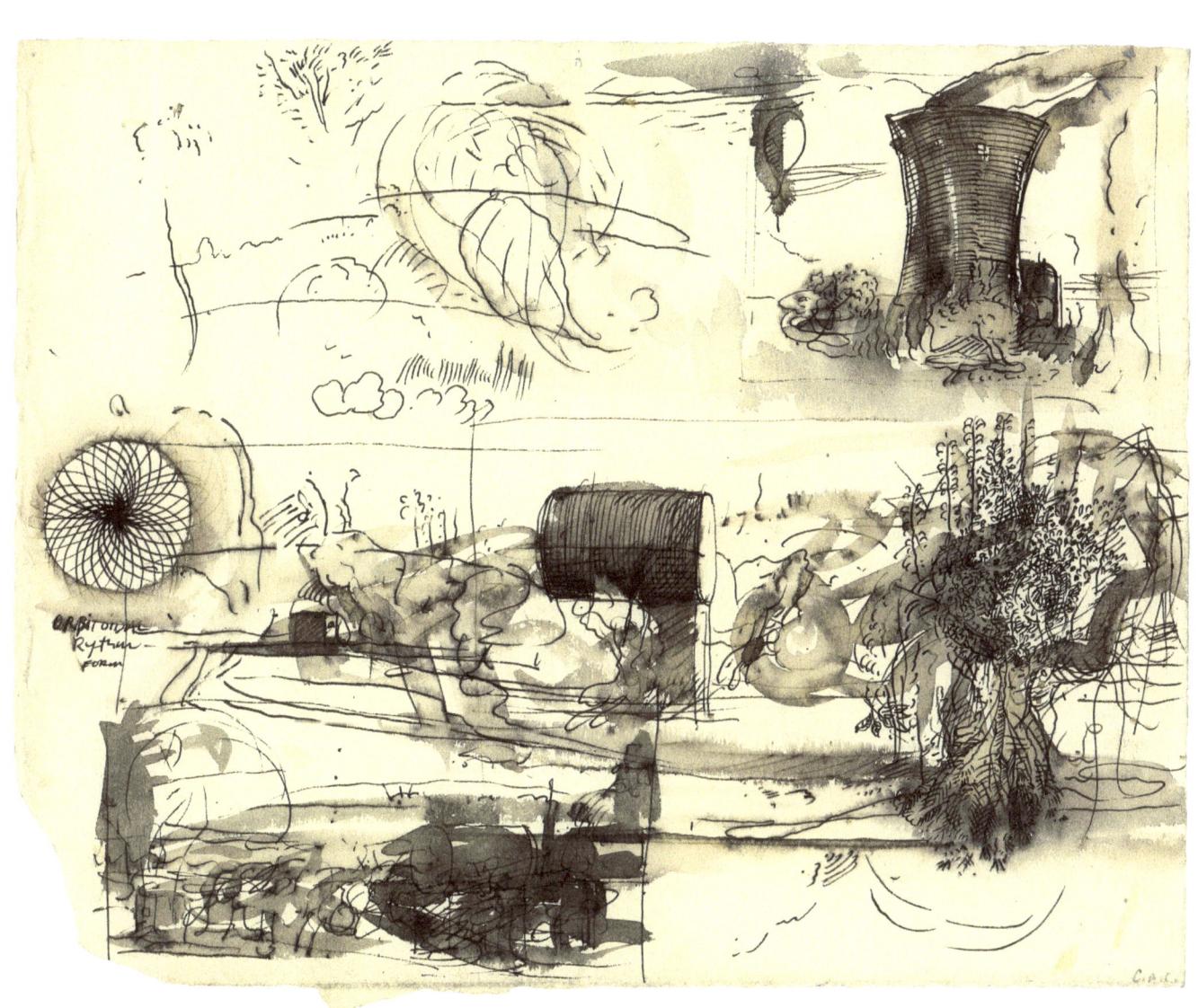

2000 - 2009

Back Yard w/ Rose Bush & Kids, 2005, Charcoal, Conte Crayon and Pencil on Paper, 15 x 11 inches

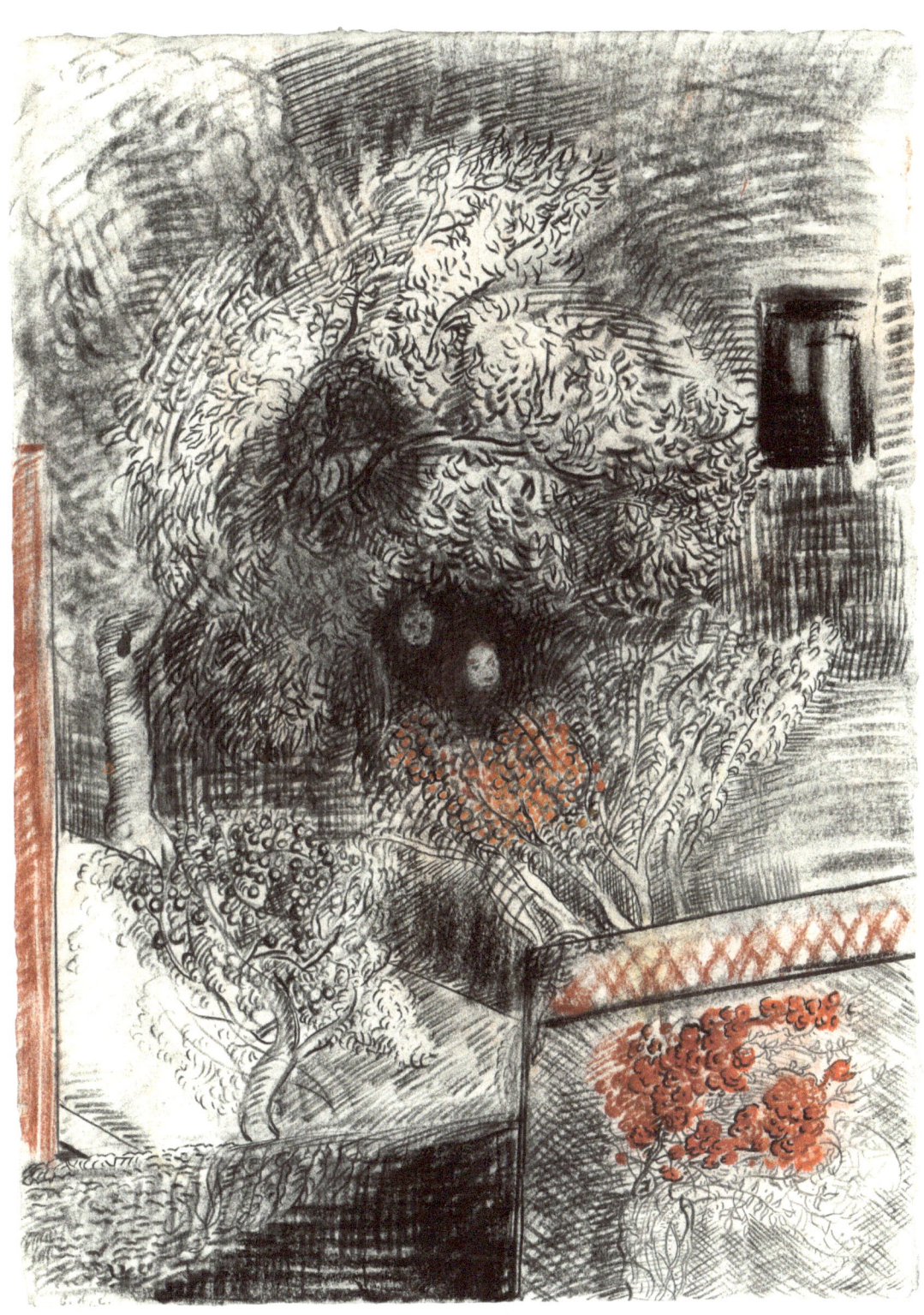

Working Drawing (w/ five), 2008 – 2009, Charcoal, Conte Crayon and Pencil on Paper, 11 x 15 inches

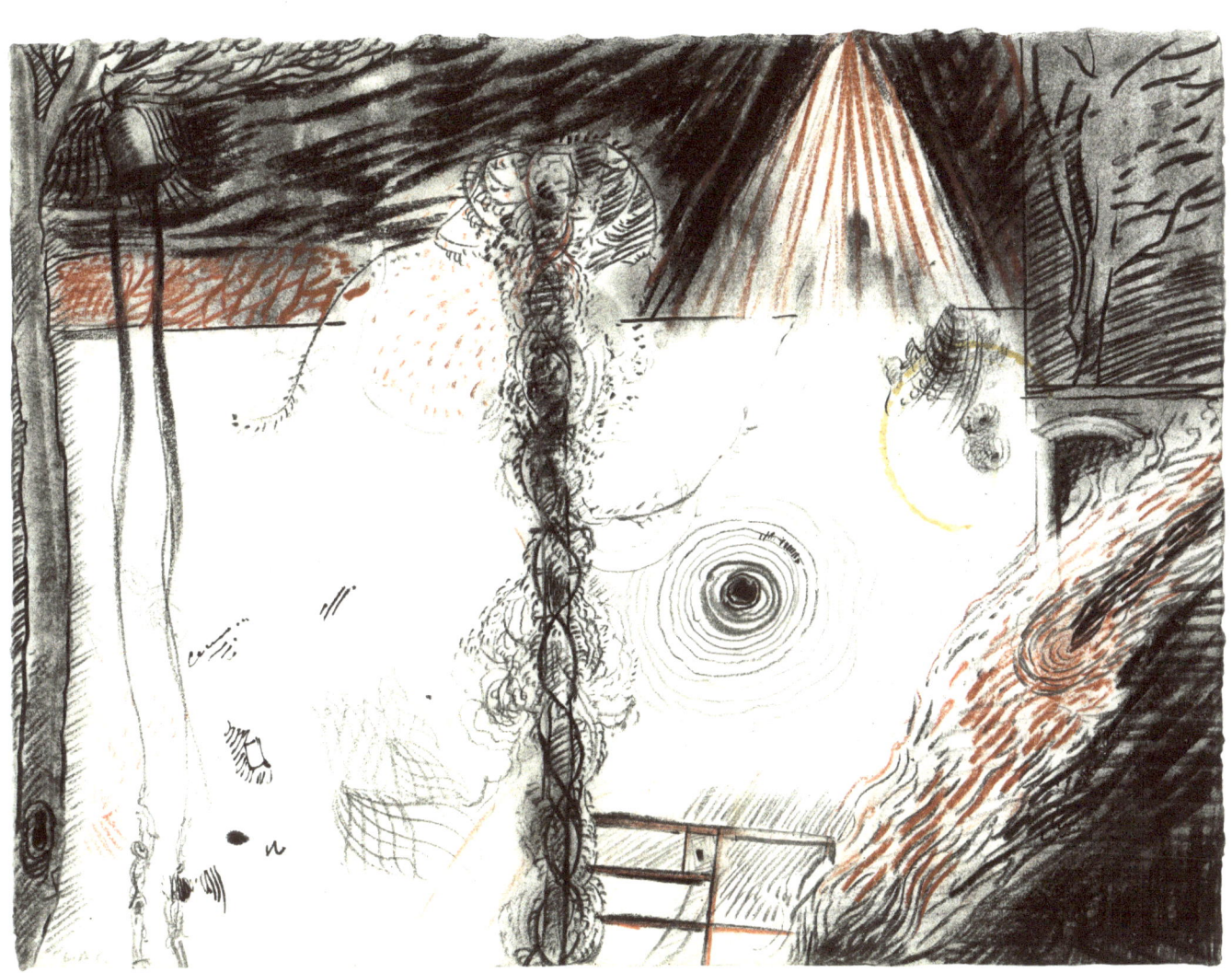

B.Y. NY Objects (antique head), 2000, Charcoal and Pencil on Paper, 11 x 15 inches

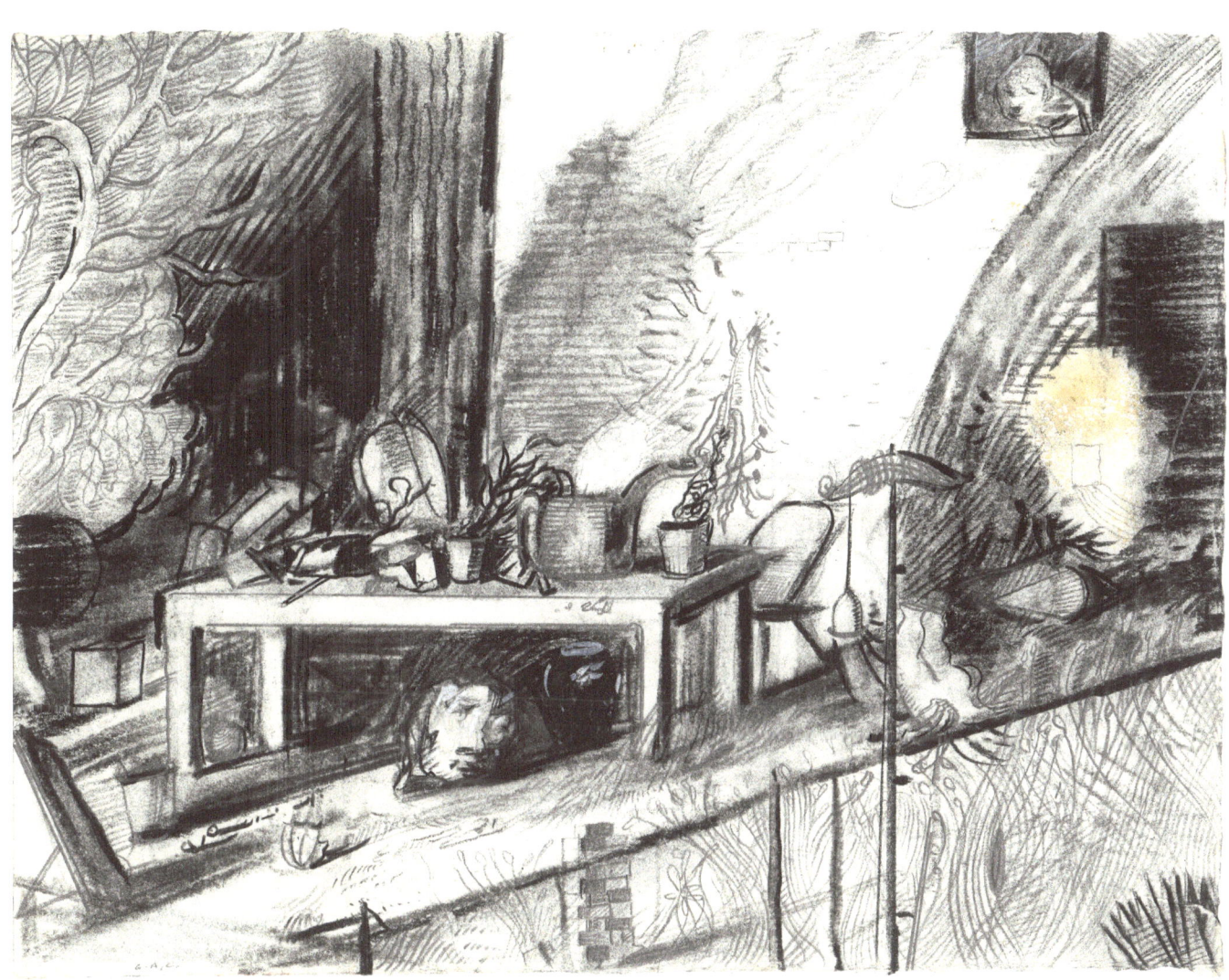

Working Farm w/ Ruins, 2002, Charcoal and Conte Crayon on Paper, 11 x 15 inches

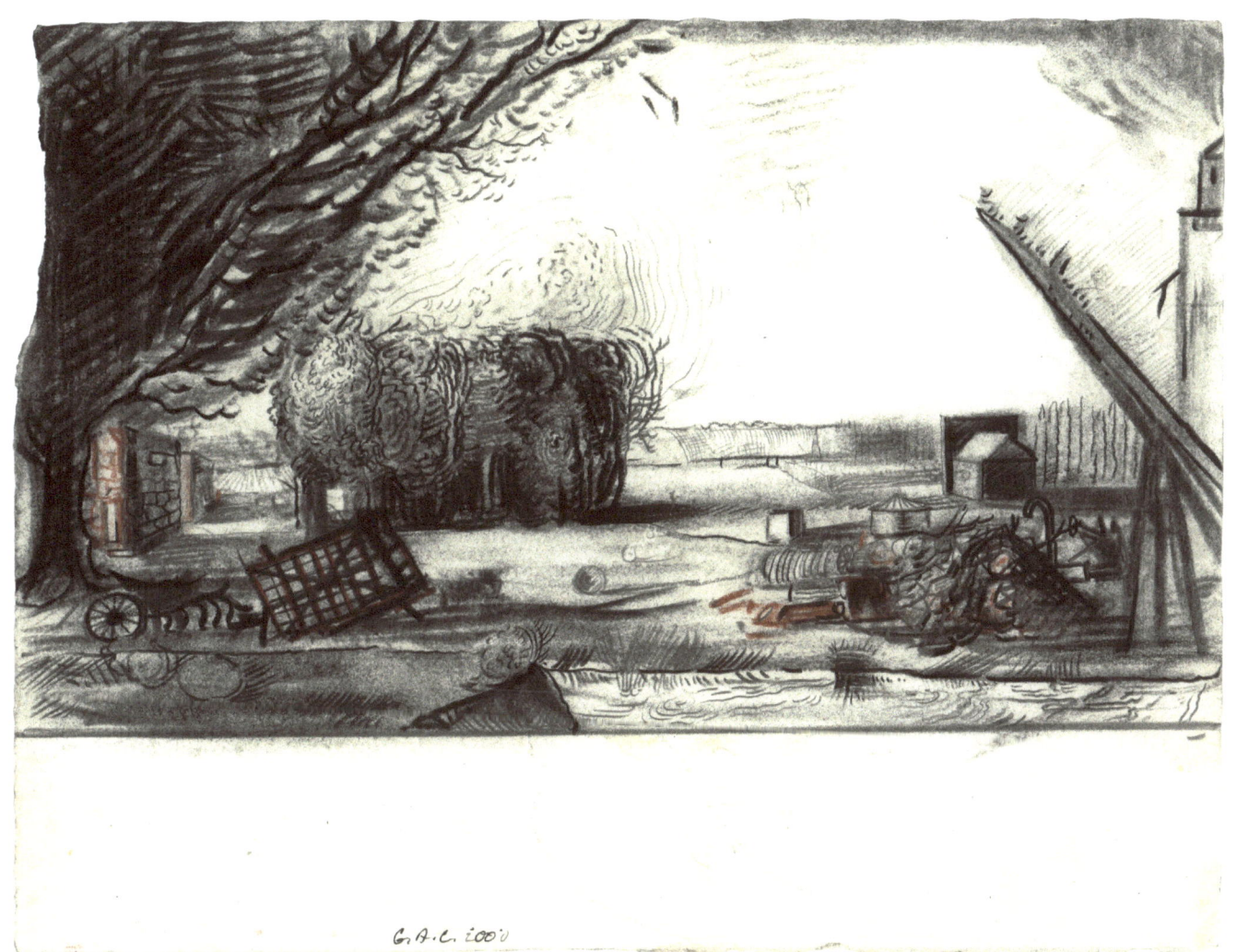

G.A.C. 2000

Working Farm w/ Ruins, 2002, Charcoal and Conte Crayon on Paper, 11 x 15 inches

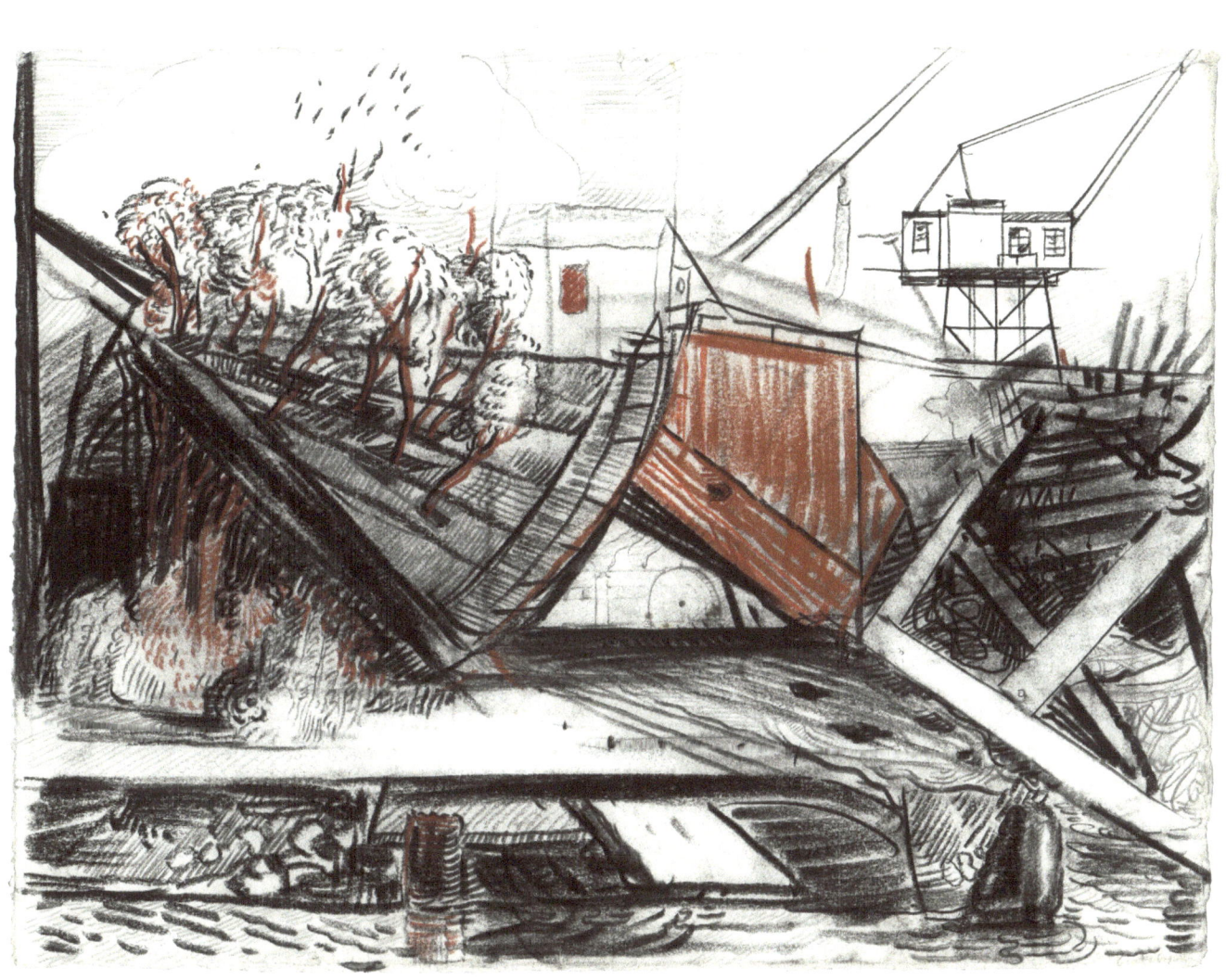

Study for Pumpkin Patch, 2007, Ink on Paper, 12 x 9 inches

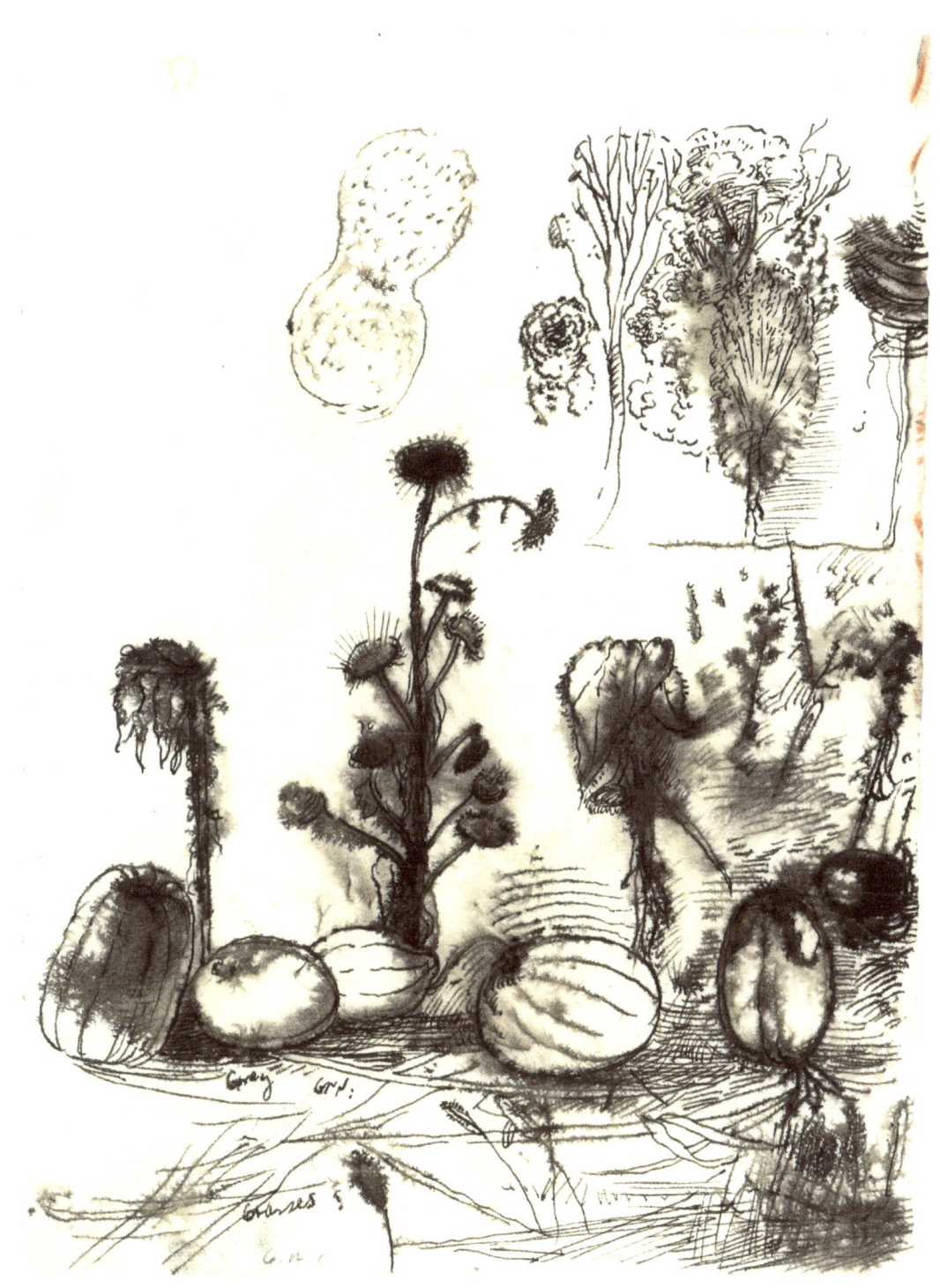

Road Trip – from I-80, 2008, Charcoal, Conte Crayon, Pastel and Pencil on Paper, 14 x 9.5 inches

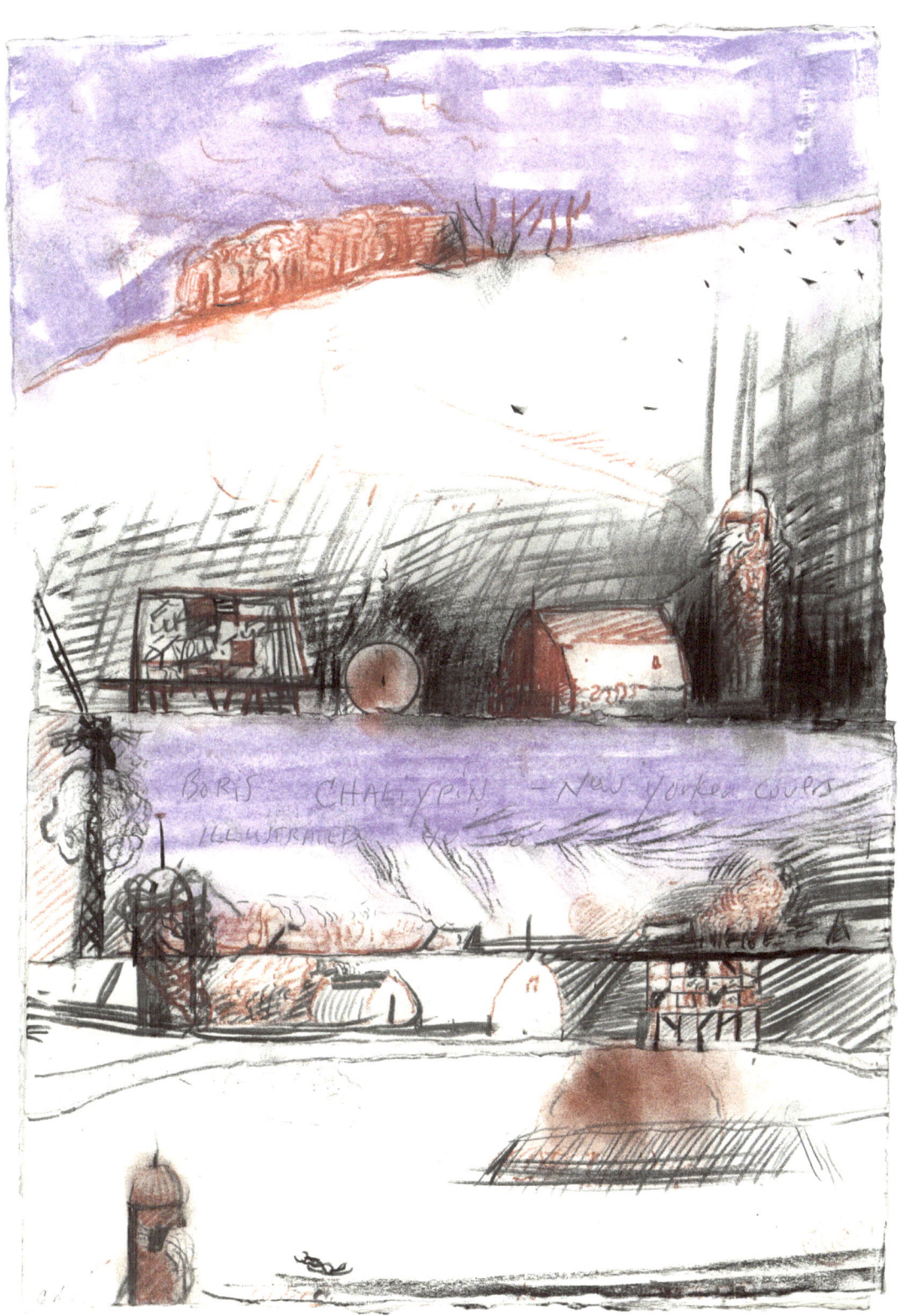

BORIS   CHALIYPIN — NEW YORKER COVERS
ILLUSTRATED

Bone Entrance to Grove, 2009, Charcoal, Pencil and Conte Crayon on Paper, 11 x 15 inches

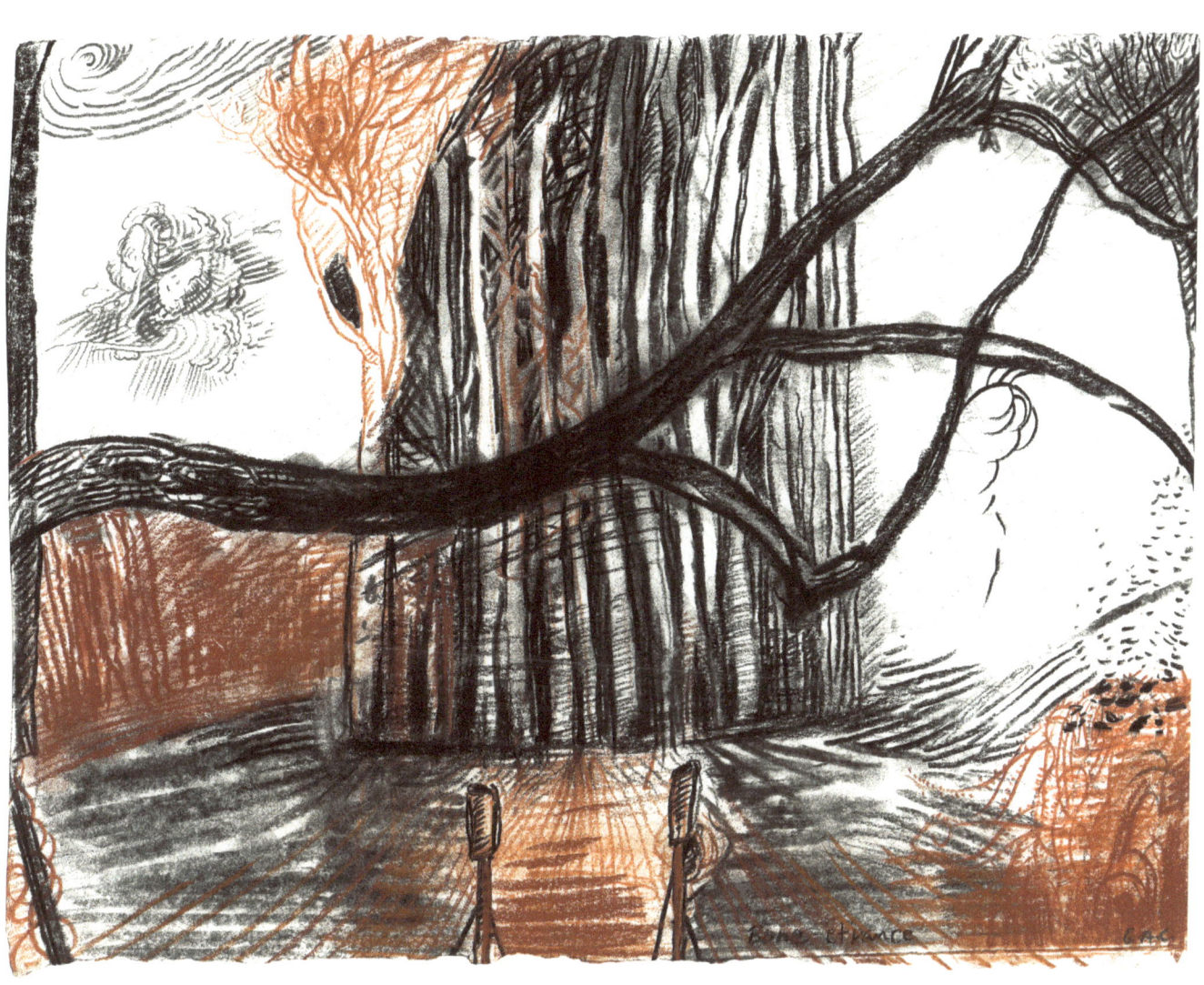

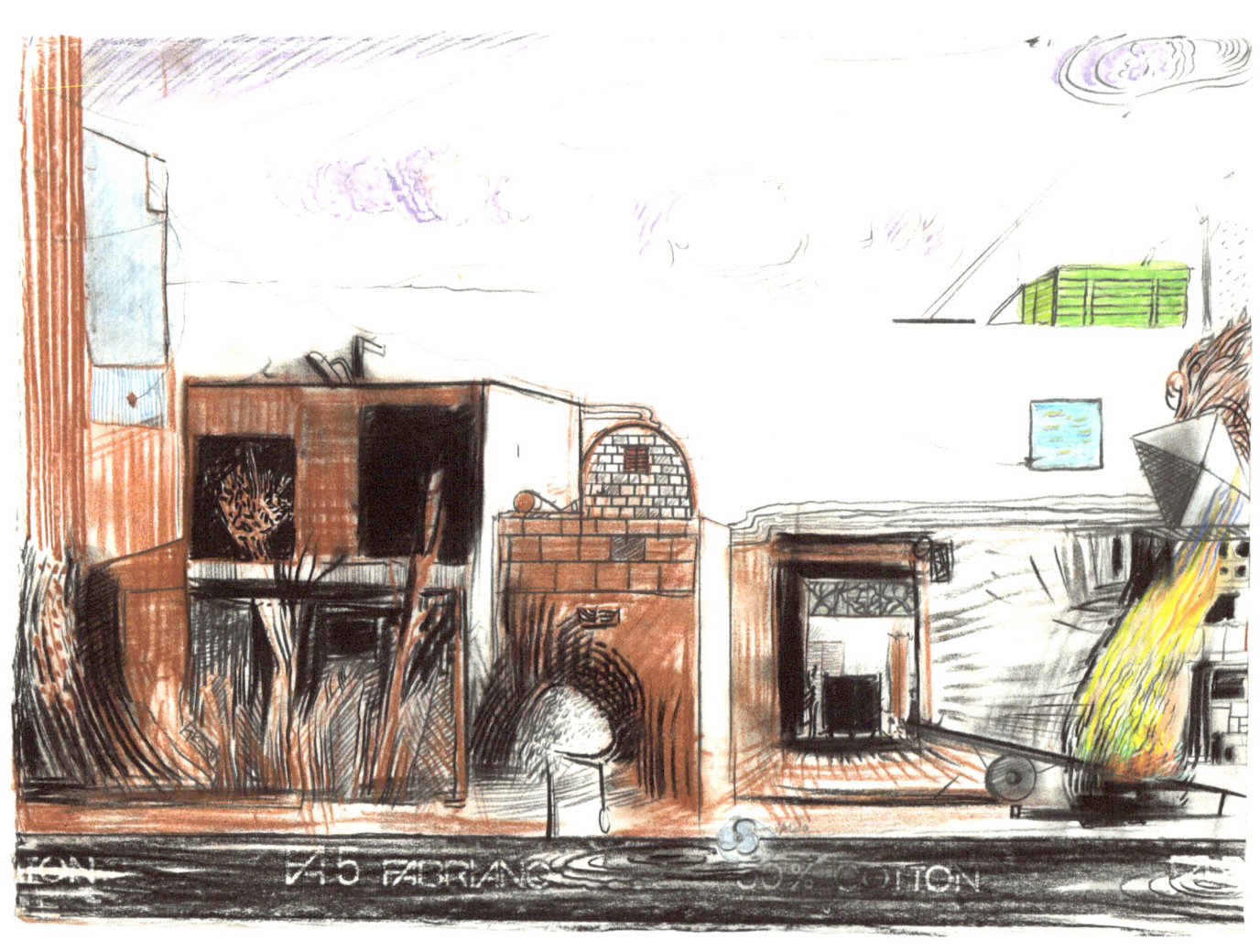

Red Hook Ruins (diptych), 2009, Charcoal, Conte Crayon, Pastel and Pencil on Paper, 14 x 40 inches

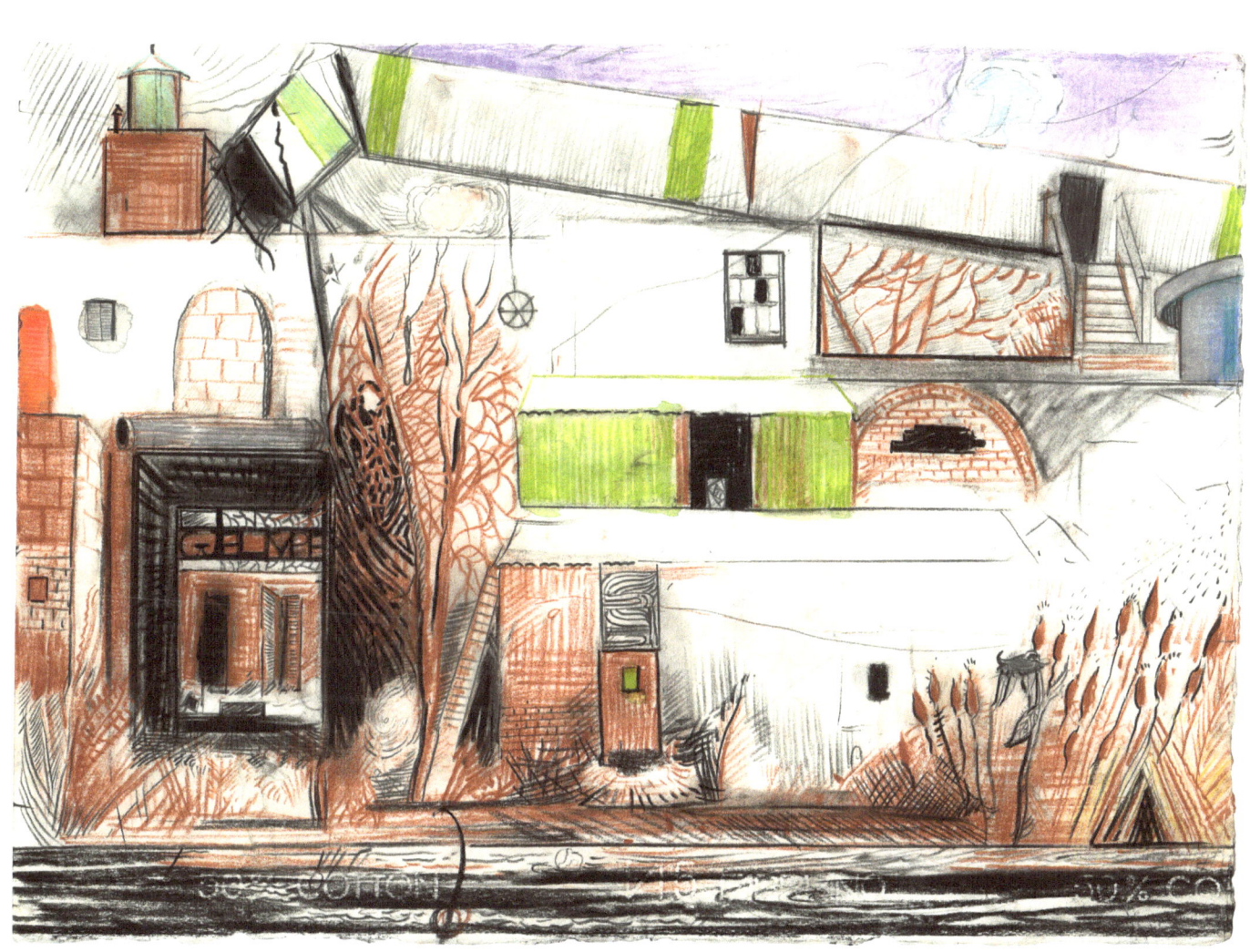

Gregory Crane

Born

1951   Bremerton, WA

Education

1975   BFA, University of Utah, Salt Lake City, UT
1976-80   The Art Students League, New York, NY

Solo Exhibitions

2004   Gregory Crane: Gardens and Vistas, Hirschl & Adler Modern, New York, NY
2000   List Gallery, Swarthmore College, Swarthmore, PA
1998   Cheryl Pelavin Fine Art, New York, NY
1996   The Southern Vermont Art Center, Manchester, VT
1991   Edward Thorp Gallery, New York, NY
1988   Edward Thorp Gallery, New York, NY
1985   Edward Thorp Gallery, New York, NY
1983   Daedalus Fine Art, Minneapolis, MN
1982   East 7th Street Gallery, New York, NY
                Interiors & Landscapes, Gallery 120, New York, NY

Group Exhibitions

2009   Drawings 1979 - 2009, Cheryl Pelavin Fine Art, NY, NY
2008   Ultra–Concentrated Joy, Ecstatic Drawings by Contemporary Artists,
                New York Academy of Art, NY, NY
                Repositioning the Landscape, Westport Arts Center, Westport, CT
2007   Neo-Integrity, Derek Eller Gallery, NY, NY
                The Missing Peace: Artists Consider the Dalai Lama, Everything
                I Do Always Comes Back To Me, S.V.A. Visual Arts Gallery, NY, NY
                25 Years of Pelavin Editions, Cheryl Pelavin Gallery, NY, NY
2003   Look Up! Contemplating the Skies, New York Academy of Sciences,
                New York, NY
                Works on Paper, The Park Avenue Armory, Hirschl & Adler Modern, NY, NY
                Chicago Arts Fair, Chicago, Ill. – Hirschl & Adler Modern, NY, NY
                The Burbs, DFN Gallery, New York, NY
2001   Verging on Real, Glyndor Gallery, Wave Hill, NY
                C M C Gallery, Santa Fe, NM
1998   Artists Choose Artists, The Century Association, New York, NY
                Divining Nature, Southeast Center for Contemporary Art,
                Winston - Salem, NC
                The New Metropolis - A Century of Greater New York, 1898-1998,
                Museum of the City of New York, NY
                Cheryl Pelavin Fine Art, New York, NY
1997   P.P.O.W. Gallery, New York, NY
1996   The Paine Webber Collection, Museum of Fine Arts, Boston, MA
                Annual Summer Watercolor Exhibition, P.P.O.W. Gallery, New York, NY
                Following the Light-The Artist and Their Teacher,
                G.C. Lucas Gallery, Indianapolis, IN
                The Modern Landscape, Queens Borough Library Gallery, NY
1995   Re-Presenting Representation II, Arnot Art Museum, Elmira, NY
                Winter Gallery Group Exhibition, Edward Thorp Gallery, New York, NY

1994	Summer Gallery Group Exhibition, Edward Thorp Gallery, New York, NY

1994   Summer Gallery Group Exhibition, Edward Thorp Gallery, New York, NY
Mountains of the Mind, The Aspen Art Museum, Aspen, CO
Arabesque, PPOW Gallery, New York, NY

1993   Landscape as Metaphor, Fitchburg Art Museum, CT
Visceral Landscapes, Travel without Boundaries, Carl Hammer Gallery,
Chicago, IL
Twilight Intervals, Patricia Shea Gallery, Santa Monica, CA
Gallery Group Exhibition, Edward Thorp Gallery, New York, NY
Growth and Atrophy: The Empathetic Landscape, School 33 Art Center,
Baltimore, MD
Beyond Description: Visions of Nature, G.W. Einstein Gallery,
New York, NY

1992   Edward Thorp Gallery, New York, NY

1991   Getting Away, Champion Gallery, Champion International Corp., Stamford, CT
Art for Your Collection, The Rhode Island School of Design, Providence, RI
The Natural Perception, The Gallery at Hastings-on-Hudson,
Hastings-on-Hudson, NY
1991 Invitational, The New Britain Museum of Art, New Britain, CT
Edward Thorp Gallery, New York, NY

1990   The Unique Print: '70 into '90, Museum of Fine Arts, Boston, MA
Intaglio Printing in the 1980's, The Zimmerli Art Museum, Rutgers
University, New Brunswick, NJ
Somewhere (curated by Robert Mahoney Lintas), Worldwide at One Dag
Hammarskjold Plaza, New York, NY
Harmony & Discord: American Landscape Today, Virginia
Museum of Fine Arts, Richmond, VA
Summer, Edward Thorp Gallery, New York, NY

1989   The Unquiet Landscape, Frumkin/Adams Gallery, New York, NY
The Unquiet Landscape: Recent Expressionist & Fantasy Landscape Paintings
(curated by Allan Frumkin), The Arts Club of Chicago, IL
Prints of the 1980's, National Gallery of Art, Washington, DC
Summer, Edward Thorp Gallery, New York, NY
Nocturnal Visions in Contemporary Painting, Whitney Museum of American Art at
The Equitable Center, New York, NY
Landscape, Betsy Rosenfield Gallery, Chicago, IL
Contemporary Environment Art, Advisory Service of the Museum of Modern Art,
General Electric Company, Fairfield, CT
New American Landscape, Fay Gold Gallery, Atlanta, GA

1988   Landscape Anthology, Grace Borgenicht Gallery, New York, NY
Edward Thorp Gallery, New York, NY
Imprimatur, North Carolina Museum of Art, Raleigh, NC

1987   Monotypes II, Allan Frumkin Gallery, New York, NY
Edward Thorp Gallery, New York, NY
The American Landscape, Met Life Gallery, New York, NY

1987   Utopian Visions, Art Advisory Service of the Museum of Modern Art,
American Express Corporate Headquarters, New York, NY

1986   Landscapes: Real & Imagined, Squibb Gallery, Princeton, NJ

1986   Night Landscapes, Schreiber/Cutler Gallery, New York, NY
The American Landscape, Elliot Smith Gallery, St. Louis, MO
Edward Thorp Gallery, New York, NY

1985   Nocturnal Images, The Pain Art Center & Arboretum, Oshkosh, WI;
Burpee Art Museum, Rockford, IL
Landscape, Seascape, Cityscape, 1960-1985, Contemporary Arts Center, New Orleans, LA

	Places Here and Now, Greenville County Museum of Art, Greenville, SC
	Edward Thorp Gallery, New York, NY
1984	P.S. 122, New York, NY
	The Center Gallery, New York, NY
	Jan Cicero Gallery, Chicago, IL
	Portraits, Gracie Mansion Gallery, New York, NY
	Semaphore Gallery, New York, NY
	Innovative Landscapes, Holly Solomon Gallery, New York, NY
	Edward Thorp Gallery, New York, NY
	Painting and Sculpture Today, Indianapolis Museum of Art, IN
	The Natural Site: Landscapes Now, Park Avenue Atrium, New York, NY
1983	Artist's Space, New York, NY
	Edward Thorp Gallery, New York, NY
	Landscape, The William Paterson College of New Jersey, Wayne, NJ
	Painting New York, Museum of the city of New York, NY
1982	East 7th Street Gallery, New York, NY
1980	Gallery of the Southwest, Taos, NM
1978	Salt Lake City Arts Center, Salt Lake City, UT
	Aisling Gallery, New York, NY
	Timothy Blackburn Gallery, New York, NY
1976	1976-1981, The Art Student's League of New York, NY
1975	University of Utah Museum of Fine Arts, Salt Lake City, UT

Awards

1983	The MacDowell Colony Fellowship
1981	The MacDowell Colony Fellowship

Teaching

1990-Present	School of Visual Arts, New York, NY
	Instructor in Painting

Bibliography

Victoria Donohoe, Philadelphia Inquirer (September 13, 2000).
Carl Little," Gregory Crane at Cheryl Pelavin," Art in America (July 1999).
April Gornik, "Gregory Crane - The Four Seasons," Bomb Magazine (Spring 1999).
Ken Johnson, The New York Times (November 27,1998).
Ken Johnson, The New York Times, Art Guide (December 18, 1998).
Ken Johnson, The New York Times, Art Guide (December 4, 1998).
"What's Up Downtown," Downtown Express (December 1998).
Dominique Nahas, "The Modern Landscape," Art Review (September 15, 1996).
Elizabeth Wilson, "Arts Extra," Bennington Banner (August 16, 1996).
Simon Lane, Bomb Magazine (Spring 1994).
Roberta Smith, "PPOW", The New York Times (February 25, 1994).
Jerry Salz, "Let Us Now Praise Artist's Artists," Art & Auction (April 1993).
Louise Sheldon, The Baltimore Chronicle (March 1993, Vol. 20, No. 12).
John Dorsey, The Sun [Baltimore, MD] (February 24, 1993).
Bomb Magazine (Fall 1992).
Vivian Raynor, The New York Times (October 13, 1991).
Robert Mahoney, Arts (September 1991).
Vivian Raynor, "Accent is on the Abstract in a New Britain Landscape Show,"
The New York Times (February 17, 1991).
Laura Cloud, Art New England (April/May, 1991).

Kelli Pryor, "Back to Nature," Avenue (February 1989).
Cathleen McGuigan, "Transforming the Landscape," Newsweek
(December 26,1988).
Carl Little, "Gregory Crane at Edward Thorp," Art in America (November 1988).
Deborah Solomon, "Back to Nature," House & Garden (November 1988).
"Press Guide 88: Best Picture," New York Press (September 30, 1988).
Robert Mahoney, "Regional Paradise," New York Press (May 20, 1998).
Roberta Smith, "Gregory Crane," The New York Times (May 20, 1998).
Linda Nochlin, "En Plein Air: Recent Views of the Great Outdoors,"
Interview (April 1988).
Gerrit Henry, "Night Landscapes, Schriber/Cutler," ART News (January 1987).
Timothy Cohrs, "Hudson River Editions, Pelavin Editions -- A Report Back From
The Other World of Printmaking," Arts (November 1986).
Barry Schwabsky, "R.L. Kaplan, Gregory Crane, June Leaf," Arts (September 1985).
Kendra Hamilton, "Show Displays Artists' Sense of 'Place'," The Greenville News
(August 20, 1985).
John Russell, "Gregory Crane, R.L. Kaplan, June Leaf," The New York Times
(May 24, 1985).
Willy Clay, "Gregory Crane," Arts (December 1984).
Grace Glueck, "New York Through the Eyes of Artists," The New York Times
(October 14, 1983).

Selected Collections

Amerada Hess Corporation, Houston, TX
Art Bank Program, Washington, DC
Bank of America, New York, NY
Beechwood Corporation, OH
Champion International, Stamford, CT
Chase Manhattan Bank, New York, NY
J.P. Morgan Chase, New York, NY
Chemical Bank, New York, NY
Citibank Corporation, New York, NY
Marshall Erdman, WI
Fidelity Finance, Boston, MA
Daniel & Rita Fraad, New York, NY
John Hauberg, Seattle, WA
Knight Landesman, New York, NY
McDonalds Corporation, USA
M. I. T. List Visual Art Center, MI
Millbank, Tweed, Hadley, Mclow, NY
Museum of the City of New York, NY
New Britain Museum of Art, CT
Orlando Museum, FL
Pfizer Incorporated, New York, NY
Prudential Insurance, New York, NY
Reader's Digest Association, NY
Rutgers Archive, New Brunswick, NJ
Shearson/ Lehman Brothers, New York, NY
Joshua P. Smith, Washington, DC
Edward Thorp, New York, NY
Paine Webber Corporation, New York, NY

in memory of Mom & Dad

www.ingramcontent.com/pod-product-compliance
Lightning Source LLC
Chambersburg PA
CBHW050731180526
45159CB00003B/1187